HOMEBOY
SCHOLARS

Also by Hilary Paul McGuire

Hopie and the Los Homes Gang: A Gangland Primer, 1979

Homeboys in College: Heralds of Progress, 1984

Hopie and the Los Homes Gang: A Gangland Primer,
Second Edition, 2012

Tennis Saves: Stewart Orphans Take World by Racket, 2012

Homeboys in College: Heralds of Progress,
Second Edition, 2014

HOMEBOY SCHOLARS

BREAKING THE MOLD

Hilary Paul McGuire

ISBN: 8777397195
ISBN-13: 979-8777397195

Printed in the United States of America

This book is dedicated to the aspirations of all homeboys and homegirls. Let "Homegirl Scholars" be next.

Contents

Front cover photo: Juan Carlos Jimenez-Cruz receiving two AA degrees from San Diego City College at Spreckels Organ Pavilion in Balboa Park

Back cover photo: Hilary Paul McGuire visiting Jose Cortez in Phoenix

FOREWORD
by Fr. Greg Boyle, S.J.

We were flying home from Boston. Two homies, Brandon and Saul, from enemy gangs, who work side by side in our Homeboy Bakery, were traveling with me. We gave four talks in Washington, DC, as well as Worcester and Shrewsbury, MA. They spoke about their experiences growing up in challenging situations and told their audiences about arriving at Homeboy Industries, the largest gang intervention, rehab, and re-entry program on the planet.

They told stories of their childhood with searing images of abandonment, terror, abuse, and even torture. If their stories had been flames, you'd have to keep your distance otherwise you'd get scorched. I would not have survived a single day of either of their childhoods.

As they inhabited their stories, more and more, their audiences began to stand in awe at what these two men had carried, rather than stand in judgment at how they'd carried it. Their audiences laughed, cried, and greeted their stories with resounding and standing ovations.

With each telling, they added nuance, image, and compelling details that presented their stories as a true light...that the rest of us could see by.

As we were flying home to Los Angeles, Brandon, near the window seat was snoring and out cold. Saul, who had only been at Homeboy for six months after completing a prison stint of nine years, leans in to confide in me. "You know, G...I'm thinkin' I want to learn more...how to talk fancy."

"Yeah?" I say to him.

"Yeah," he says, "You know...what's that language they be speakin'...you know...where they leave the house, and turn around to their family...and say, 'Ta-Ta'?"

"Um," I say, "I don't know...English? ...British?"

I knew exactly what he meant. "Talk fancy" was a deepening of his story and a precision in telling it. It highlighted the nobility and dignity he felt in articulating who he was in front of people. He liked how it felt and wanted to grow more articulate, more compelling, and more certain of the truth of his story. Talk fancy. People will listen if you do this, if you grow in this, and if you inhabit your story more and more.

In the stories you will read here, you will meet folks who have come to know their sagas, to tell their histories, and who have discovered, quite unexpectedly, that they are the heroes of their stories. They aren't exactly chronicles of "bad choices" but rather journeys of undeniable truths and unshakeable goodness...where not all choices are created equal and lives can be derailed beyond one's power to safeguard them. Once you marinate your heart with these stories, you will recognize that we are all born wanting the same things. We come to see that we all belong to each other. We are human beings. We all share the same last name: Beings.

These tender stories invite us to celebrate our shared humanity and give birth to a compassion that resembles the heart of God. What gets recounted in these pages leads us to advance God's dream come true: a community of beloved belonging, where no one is left out. We can be consoled then by the fact that inclusion is our highest aspiration and there remains no "other" and no "them." It is just "us" in kinship—all of us connected in exquisite mutuality. We marvel then at the power we have, collectively, as we choose, together…to "talk fancy."

Fr. Gregory Boyle, S.J.
Founder and Executive Director of Homeboy Industries
November 26, 2021

PREFACE

How did a gringo from Oklahoma spiral into writing a trilogy about Mexican American homeboys?

In 1971, I found myself teaching both math and tennis to Chicano youth at Our Lady of Lourdes School in the heart of East LA where I was known as *Hermano Hilario*. As a brother of the Catholic Church in the Order of St. Benedict at that time, I had been sent from my monastery in Oklahoma to teach in the junior high.

While I was teaching tennis in the schoolyard, neighborhood tweens Hopie, Fernando, and Efren insinuated themselves into the group. I welcomed them despite warnings from adults, even the church pastor. Thus, I met what soon became the Los Homes Gang in the territory of the older members of the long-established Li'l Valley Gang.

I never thought I'd write a book, but what transpired prompted me to write *Hopie and the Los Homes Gang: A Gangland Primer*. My purpose in writing their story was to motivate them to read as well as to encourage adults to guide and embrace such youth rather than fear and scorn them.

Later, having parted from the monastery after 20 years, I moved to San Diego and was teaching math at San Diego City College. It happened that a judge told a clique of homies, Freddie, Smiley, Topo and Chango, to go to college or go to jail.

There they were in my class. I wrote *Homeboys in College: Heralds of Progress*, telling their story and how they inspired me to help others to get into college. It ended with my suggestion that the next book could be written by the homies themselves.

Years later, in 2016, a lady named Maria got both of my homeboy books at San Diego's Prop 47 Justice and Resource Fair. A month later, Adrian Caceres called me, explaining that he had a club at East LA College called Homeboy Scholars. He asked me to donate eight copies of each book for the club. This was how club president Gilbert Vasquez read the books and decided to call me. He suggested that I put their stories together into a new book with the club's title.

So here it is, *Homeboy Scholars: Breaking the Mold*, the fulfilment of my dreams and the conclusion of a Cholo trilogy. My wife and I have personally met most of these fine men. I'm blessed to help bring their autobiographies to the world.

INTRODUCTION

This book contains brief autobiographies of ten men. Nine have experienced many incarcerations. One is still a lifer. Six are current or former student-members of the Homeboy Scholars club of East Los Angeles College. Some have utilized the programs at Homeboy Industries, the world's largest and most unique self-help organization. Four others come from other routes. Several were born in Mexico. All are leading productive and admirable lives today.

The number of homeboys with stories of success could fill a much larger book, but this edition aspires to be a representative sampling to give readers hope and ideas they can build upon.

It starts with the story of Jose Cortez whose life gives a historical perspective. It spans immigration, the rise of Chicanismo with Cesar Chavez, and several subsequent facets of Mexican American life—all the way to retirement and an introspective survey of raising grandchildren.

The stories here include one by Gilbert Vasquez who, along with Adrian Caceres, spearheaded the production of this volume. The tales are told by the men themselves and are only minimally edited for clarity. Enjoy and share these words of encouragement with others.

1 JOSE CORTEZ

We came to this country in 1951. My father was killed in an accident. That left my mother, my sister and me: Jose Cortez. Back in those days, it was difficult for single women to work. My mother really had nothing she could rely on. No one wanted to hire her to work in the fields. We decided to make the journey north: *para el norte.*

We crossed the border at El Paso when I was three years old. Soon after that, my mom met a gentleman who was also a farm worker and who was single. They hooked up. The whole family was approached by a contractor to work in the sugar beet fields in Colorado. Having no documentation, we figured that would be the ideal place to get away from the border.

We joined the caravan and went to Colorado, about fifty miles north of Denver, to a place called Greeley. There, my parents became field workers, working in the beets. The local Chicanos would call us *betabeleros.* There were a lot of us who came from Mexico, Texas, and New Mexico every year to work in the beet fields. We did that for a while.

Back in those days, sugar beets were the cash crop for many of the farmers in the area. Sugar beets are bigger than the variety of beets people buy in the store to eat as a vegetable. Companies like Great Western had huge refineries to make sugar from sugar beets. A lot of people don't know that. They think all sugar comes from sugar cane.

A lot of our people also went to North Dakota, Wyoming, and Nebraska to work in sugar beet fields as well as potato fields. The local people would not work in that kind of environment. It had to be the people who came from Mexico who were already adapted to working in the fields. That's how we human beings became like a product to the growers and the huge corporations which couldn't make money without us.

They started making camps for us where we could live year-round. Some of us did the camps, but it was hard because in the winter, there wasn't any work for us. We could only work in the summer. Some of the camps were warm enough, but others weren't. It just depended on where you were staying. We could deal with the cold. It was the discrimination and racism that was harder to deal with.

Because we were poor, spoke limited English, and were brown, we were the outcasts. That hardens you. The homeboys in the city were hardened too, but in a different way. We were hardened because we had to be strong to endure the physical work. On top of that, we were hardened because we had to fight our way through the school year. Every day, I would come home with a black eye or bloody nose.

I am lucky that I don't have a broken nose. I learned to duck quickly. Back then, we weren't called homeboys. We were called *pachucos* just because of our having the same ethnicity as the urban zoot suiters who devised their stylish garb during World War II. They referred to themselves as *pachucos*. I watched the older *pachucos* and learned how to fight with my feet using a kick. I became an expert at using my feet and my fists. I think that's what saved me. I never took up boxing or had a desire to learn to box. I just knew how to defend myself with street fighting.

Since we weren't making any money in the wintertime, we would follow the other migrant workers who left Colorado every year. They told us about Arizona. In 1960, my family arrived in Phoenix. It was a whole different environment. We weren't out in the rural areas anymore. But we still followed the crops, working as migrant farmworkers. Everywhere we went, we had to fight, even with our own people. We'd come to a new town and they'd say, "Hey, where you from?"

We'd say, "I don't know, man! We're migrant farmworkers."

When we were in Phoenix, working in the valleys, Cesar Chavez came and was organizing the farmworkers in the area. I didn't want to get involved because I saw what my parents went through. Mentally, I wanted to get away from the whole thing, thinking that all those ugly memories of racism and discrimination would go away. It did for me, temporarily. But I saw how the people were still being treated, so I decided to jump in because

I'm a fighter. When I decided I would help my people, the flame of activism kicked in.

At first, I was a gopher for the Cesar Chavez organizers. Later, they pulled me in to become one of the labor organizers. Then I was one of Cesar's bodyguards because, at that time, I was slim, knew how to fight, and could run fast. I could outrun the sheriff's deputies. I was always with him when he came to the Phoenix area. I didn't go to other cities when he left because there was a lot of work to be done in Phoenix. We had a lot of activity organizing farmworkers.

I began to see the similarities between the homeboys who lived in the city and those of us who grew up in the rural areas. We had the same mentality. We had a chip on our shoulders because we had been punched and kicked around. We were seeking an identity to belong to, but at the same time, we hadn't accepted the fact that the keys to our salvation were spirituality and education.

Education came first for me and after that came spirituality. Education came because of Cesar. He saw that I had potential and said, "I'm gonna get you a grant to go to broadcasting school." He got me a $5000 grant to go to the Ron Bailie School of Broadcasting in Phoenix in around 1979 or 1980. I got my jump start in the media by going to broadcasting school. I was at the right place at the right time. I couldn't speak English or Spanish correctly, but Cesar still saw the potential in me. He said, "One day, I'm gonna have my own radio station and you can work for me."

I said, "I'm glad you believe that, because I sure don't."

He said, "You know that you believe it too."

I followed his advice. While going to school, in addition to my schoolwork, I would work on my English. I'd buy a newspaper every night and with a cheap little tape recorder, I'd record myself as I read the paper out loud. Then I'd play it back and listen to how I made mistakes in pronouncing words. I'd say, "That's not how you say it! It's not 'jis,' it's 'just'!" I started to correct myself. It took me a while to learn how to speak English correctly, but I knew that if I was going to survive in this country, I had to be able to navigate within the system.

After broadcasting classes, I took courses in public speaking and acting so I could speak in front of crowds and not be afraid.

I got a job as part of the first bilingual radio program in Phoenix in 1980.

That's how I got my start in education.

As for as the spirituality, I had always had an affinity for the Native American culture. I started to learn about the greatness of our ancestors and how they were in touch with the earth and lived in harmony with nature. I met with people who had the same philosophy. I did sweat lodges and the tipi ceremonies which are the peyote ceremonies. A tipi, often confused with a teepee, is distinguished by having smoke flaps at the top. Anyway, I decided to become a sun dancer.

For this, we go up into the mountains, fast from food and water for four days, and start dancing. At the end, they cut your chest, put pegs in and hang you from a tree. When you are done praying, you don't just pull the pegs out. You gotta rip them out. It leaves permanent scars. All these years, I was looking for Jesus Christ and I found the Creator in a tree.

When I retired from my first radio job, I became media man and director of public relations for the Phoenix headquarters of *Chicanos por La Causa*. I did that for 20 years. After that, I did media fundraisers for various community organizations, things like oldies dances, food pantries, car shows, and bookmobiles, anything to promote education and guide young people and the whole community in positive directions.

During the pandemic, while being isolated at home away from many friends and family all over the United States and Mexico, I had time to profoundly analyze my life. At 73, I'm entering a new passage in life: embracing the beauty of being a grandparent. No more working in the fields, going to school, fighting for social justice, being a radio announcer, DJing events, and staying up late. However, I will continue running as long as the Creator allows me, since that will help me to stay healthy to keep up with the grandkids.

Grandchildren, though a great joy to many, can be exhausting. However, time together can give you a renewed sense of purpose and motivate you to take better care of yourself. Your grandchildren can help you stay sharp, be more active, and live longer. Being a grandparent is a gift from the Creator.

There is a spiritual connection between a grandparent and a grandchild. Rupturing this can cause great emotional pain and suffering. As a three-year-old child, I was separated from my grandmother. To this day I can think back and remember the pain which that separation caused me. It also damaged me physically, causing me to develop a stuttering problem that lasted several years.

Our most important and sacred role as a grandparent involves cultivating our grandchildren's spiritual development. Parents cultivate their children's spirits too, but grandparents' teachings have a special quality that supplements, not replaces, a parent's teachings. Acting as a spiritual guide involves teaching your grandchildren to harvest such fruits of the spirit as love, tolerance, compassion, reverence, joy, peace, gentleness, goodness, faith, and kindness. These tangible and intangible qualities are related to the deepest and most mysterious dimensions of your relationship with your grandchildren.

There is a natural tendency for the young to give credence to the spiritual powers of the elderly. Various religions have accorded to elders the power of blessing (*bendición*). I will always remember my grandmother asking me to kneel in front of her so that she could bless me and ask the Creator to watch over me. Now I do the same thing with my grandchildren when I bless them.

When I finish talking with the Creator, I turn to my grandchildren and say, "Come *mijo/mija.*" I put my hands lightly on the tops of their heads and begin by thanking the Creator for helping them. I will specifically mention their struggles during that week and tell the Creator something about them that the child will know to be true. If they have made mistakes during the week, I will mention their honesty in telling the truth. If they failed, I specifically mention my appreciation of how hard they have tried. If they have taken even a short nap without a nightlight, I can celebrate their bravery of sleeping in the dark. Then I give them my blessing and ask the spirits of our ancestors and all the good people of the centuries past to watch over them.

Grandparents are uniquely suited to connect with their grandchildren in a contemplative state of mind. Both are naturally primed to marvel at and evaluate the mysteries of the universe in a profound manner. By so doing, we grandparents illuminate and transform ourselves for the better. *Como Siempre, La Voz de Aztlan.*

A couple years ago, I did a fundraiser for the Peace and Dignity Journey. It's a spiritual run that takes place every four years. One end starts in Alaska and the other starts in the Tierra del Fuego Province in Chile. They meet in a central area. In past runs, that climax was in Mexico or Panama. This year, 2020, it will be in Ecuador. [Editor's note: the physical run was canceled for 2020 due to concerns over COVID-19.]

I am not going to run the full journey this year. But I will run with them when they pass through Arizona for about a week. It's not how far you run or how fast you run. When you run, you offer a prayer to Mother Earth. That's what it's all about.

The runs I have done are experiences I'll never forget. That's why I say that education and spirituality are the things that can save homeboys. When a homeboy comes to me for guidance, I tell him, "I don't have the magic to turn you around, but if you're willing to put out and make a sacrifice, you will change your life. You can, because you are a human being. *Sí, se puede.*"

1. Jose as a Farmworker

2. Jose on the Radio and at a Car Show

2 GILBERT VASQUEZ

I, Gilbert Vasquez, was born in LA's General Hospital in 1963. My parents and I lived in East LA on South Ferris Avenue just five blocks from Fourth Street Elementary.

My early school years went fine; I was on the student council and taking summer school every year just because I loved school. I played cello in 4th grade band and trumpet in 5th grade. I even learned to play a mean game of chess during summer school—mostly because I had a crush on a girl.

Having been baptized and taken catechism classes and First Communion at St. Benedict's Church, I was even a pretty good Catholic boy.

Unfortunately, the influence of homies my age was far stronger than any school or church teacher. One day I joined my friends who got the idea to hide in a closet after school. We were caught burglarizing Fourth Street classrooms—taking just little stuff from students' desks.

I was kicked out of the student council. The principal told my parents, and my mom beat me.

For 6th grade, I went to nearby Eastmont Intermediate for a month or two until my parents, who were both working, decided to move to Montebello for a better neighborhood.

By then, I totally scorned both band and chess. At Montebello Intermediate, I soon moved from cigarettes to weed. The principal gave me a choice between getting swats and him telling my parents. I chose the swats since I knew they would be far easier than ones my drunken father would give me.

In 7th grade, about 1976, I had my catechism classes and confirmation at St. Alphonsus Church. Unfortunately, my less spiritual but more substantial confirmation was with VNE, a gang I had long admired.

Some of my school friends were already members of the VNE Juniors. They primed me for membership by introducing me to angel dust. That's a combination of liquid phencyclidine (PCP) and dried mint leaves. Smoking that stuff was so strong that I lost my awareness. "*Chale!*" I realized I needed to be aware of my surroundings—not for school's sake, but because I had to be able to defend myself. My buddies and I settled on a less potent mix.

A Benedictine brother, Hilary McGuire, now editor of this book, was working with homies from 1971-73. He was stationed a mere three miles west of my VNE territory at Our Lady of Lourdes School in the heart of East LA. Though that sounds close, because of gang boundaries, it was more like a different country. He was working with the Li'l Valley (LV) and Los Homes gangs. LV & VNE, at least in those days, didn't get along. In homie parlance, that's *real* bad.

As I was coming up in the '70s, there was already such a longstanding animosity between VNE and LV that neither would venture into each other's territories unless well-armed and highly-stoked on lots of weed sprayed with PCP. Though I was never personally in a drive-by, some VNE dudes would load up in every sense of the word and roar through Li'l Valley, guns a-blazing. They knew which house was the LV hangout. They'd drive by and riddle the house with bullets.

I really needed my wits and awareness one night in the 8th grade. Some of my VNE *veteranos* saw a dude from a rival gang writing his *placas* on one of our barrio walls. They said to me, "Here's a knife; do something with it!"

Without hesitation, I knew what they meant, and I did it. That was the first time I ever stabbed anyone. I guess having my awareness with me didn't help that much; he stabbed me right back. I still bear the results 45 years later—along with the scars of five or six other encounters.

Those same friends who vouched for me to become a member of VNE were chosen as the ones who then jumped me into the gang. The three of them pummeled me mercilessly right there in the middle of Taylor Avenue in Montebello. Together the three punched, kicked, and tackled me. It's the kind of thing where your arms, legs, and torso are black and blue for weeks afterward. Some of your ribs get cracked and it hurts to breathe for the next three months or more. The expression is that they "beat the hell out of me," but judging by what I did for the next 30 years, it seems they beat the devil *into* me.

I still think of those guys as my friends, but I haven't seen them for years. The last I heard was that one was doing 19 years at Pelican Bay, California's only supermax prison.

When I was in high school, my problem was that I was not taking school seriously. Most of my friends and I were offered vocational courses versus ones that would require analytical thinking and problem solving. I took the ones that did not require me to do much thinking. Then I became bored with them and so complacent that I didn't really try to reach my full capacity as a student.

Now, as a college student, I have a tremendous amount of difficulty in writing papers for English classes. Students will float to the mark that they are challenged to reach. I, as a working-class student, had no one reminding me that I could accomplish whatever I set out to do.

I got kicked out of Montebello High School for possession of marijuana in 11th grade, 1981. No wonder I never could focus on learning anything. I never graduated. It was not until years later—in prison of course—that I was able to concentrate enough to get my GED.

I first went to LA County Jail (LACJ) in 1982-83 at the Biscailuz Center in Monterey Park, just north of East LA. That site was brand new at the time.

From 1982-2000, I was in and out of every one of approximately seven LACJ sites, some more than others. Well, I never made it to Sybil Brand Institute even though it was only a quarter mile down Sheriff Road from Biscailuz where I started; Sybil Brand was for women. Both are closed and repurposed now.

When I got out of Biscailuz in '83, I worked as a painter for six years. We did apartment buildings and houses, both inside and out. At first, I was still in my high-school-marijuana stage.

Then Reagan's crackdown on both the border and marijuana started being effective. That made marijuana scarce and expensive in the mid-to-late '80s. But crack was plenty cheap. It didn't take long before I was addicted to crack. I started getting laid off, then was totally fired from my paint crew.

That's when one might say that I became addicted to crime and the LACJ system—until I made it to the bigtime in 2001.

They sent me to California state prison for ADW, assault with a deadly weapon without a firearm, Penal Code 245A. Section B is "with a firearm." I got four years for that.

Once released, I returned to prison in a matter of a few months. This time I got another three years. I was out for almost a year when I returned to prison, this time with a new CDC number. From 2001-2012, I was in and out on the prison circuit.

Of course, my crack addiction had a very negative effect on my personal and family life during my various times on the outside. No one wanted to have me around. I became an outcast from my family and friends. I couldn't keep a girlfriend.

That went on all through the '90s and another 12 years into the new century. I've dated and have had more than my share of girlfriends. I had my first abortion when I was 15 and another at 25. I've never married and don't have any kids—that I know about.

In 2012 at the age of 49, I finally got sick of my life. I told my girlfriend at the time, Inez Salcedo (an amazing person who's still a great friend), "I'm tired of this life; I wanna try something different. When I come back, I'm gonna be someone else." I checked myself into healthRIGHT 360 in Westlake.

People may ask how I ever heard of a place that was 13 miles away from where I was living in Pico Rivera. I would reply, "I don't know about any place in Pico Rivera; all I know is that my parole officer gave me the option to rehab at healthRIGHT 360 or go back to jail. That was a pretty simple choice."

The State of California paid for the rehab and my dad gave me a ride. The residential rehab program lasted for six months. For some reason, healthRIGHT takes only parolees and focuses on behavioral modification. It sure worked for me. I'm evidence that the California government makes good decisions—occasionally.

The things that finally put me on the right track were the two Rs, "rehab and religion." These replaced the two Rs that I grew up with, "run and resist?" Those two always caused me to end up in the same place, *in*-for-a-long-time and *in*-carceration.

Eventually the two Rs of rehab and religion have led me to the *three* Rs. Those are the ones that kids are supposed to learn in elementary school, but which I never learned much of: reading, writing, and 'rithmetic. Why didn't I learn them? Because I was too busy resisting what my parents, teachers, priests, and religion teachers were telling me was the right way to live.

The first thing I learned about the three Rs is that the name is sort of a joke. It's a joke for kids who can't read well enough to realize that "writing" doesn't start with an R and neither does "arithmetic." Thankfully, I can *still* learn. At last I *am* learning the three Rs at community college.

I asked Charles, my counselor at rehab, how he got the job and where he went to school. Since he went to East LA College, I decided right then that I would go there too.

At ELAC, I became active in a club called Students Against Substance Abuse. Because of that, I met Romen Lopez who was president of the Associated Student Union. He convinced me to join him in student government. Like Romen, I have also been interacting with students on other campuses. One of my many contacts is the Underground Scholars club at UC Berkeley.

Meanwhile, Adrian Caceres founded Homeboy Scholars, an organization composed of around 20 *pinteras* and *pinteros* like me. The club encourages the formerly incarcerated to get their education and provides support to help them through it. When Adrian was no longer able to serve as the president, I stepped into that position.

Adrian had obtained several copies of *Homeboys in College: Heralds of Progress* in 2016. I read—and re-read—the last paragraph of that book:

I end this book, not so much with a conclusion as with a declaration. Here's to all the Heralds of Progress and also, not only to them, but to those who will come after them. Theirs will be the next story written. Perhaps they will even write it themselves.

This inspired a bunch of us in the Homeboy Scholars club to write our stories. We contacted the author, and the rest is history. Many of the stories in this book are written by our guys. We hope that young homies will avoid the "run and resist" pattern which has cost us so much misery and *very* many decades of our lives.

3. Gilbert with Adrian Caceres at Pathways to College Workshop

4. Gilbert In Addiction Studies with Ricardo Sevilla

3 JUAN CARLOS JIMENEZ-CRUZ

My name is Juan Carlos Jimenez Cruz. I am the youngest of three brothers. My father was from Salvatierra, a small town between Mexico City and Guadalajara. My mother was from a small town northeast of Guadalajara called San Juan de los Lagos. I was born in Tijuana in 1971. I am a permanent resident of the US; I have a green card.

My oldest brother died when he was a year old, so I never met him. My other brother is one year older than I am. My father died when I was three or four years old. I didn't know the details until much later.

My mother told me the story on my eighteenth birthday. My father was an independent drug dealer. He was not in the cartel since he didn't work for anybody. He died of a self-inflicted head wound. We were marked for death by the cartel and his way of protecting us was to kill himself. He shot himself in front of her. Before he did, he said, "*Antes de que un hijo de su perra madre les mate a ustedes me mato yo* [before any SOB kills you, I'd rather kill myself]."

After my father died, my mother married someone from the US Navy who turned out to be an alcoholic. We lived in Barrio Sherman, a neighborhood of San Diego. He was abusive to me and my brother. He would beat our mother very badly. When she couldn't take any more, she divorced him.

We moved to K street for a while where my brother and I went to Sherman Elementary School. After the divorce, we moved around a lot. I lived in many different low-income neighborhoods. I went from Sherman to Logan Elementary and then graduated from Baker Elementary.

Baker elementary was a predominantly black community. I had a girlfriend who was black and was using me to make her boyfriend jealous. I was OK with that, even though I would get beat up or chased after school. Her boyfriend and his minions would chase me almost every day just to try to kick my ass. Sometimes they would catch me; sometimes they couldn't. One day, the whole school showed up at my house. I just didn't go out, because I wasn't gonna be the one that got his ass kicked in front of everybody.

I bounced around a whole lot more in junior high: Pershing, Lewis, Marston, Memorial, and Horace Mann—various junior highs. We had moved to the Shelltown barrio, and I began to have far more behavioral problems and bad grades. I was very truculent with a recalcitrant attitude.

I had a lot of bad influences and grew up quickly as soon as I hit junior high at age 11. I broke into a school, delivered drugs for the dealers, and got my first tattoo. I remember at Pershing Junior High School, there were big gang fights between the Market Street Boys and the Encanto Boys.

During the summers, I often visited the *"barrio la muerta"* where my father died. That's in Colonia Libertad, the Liberty neighborhood of Tijuana. My mom would send me to stay there with my uncle and cousins whenever I got into trouble.

I was never in any gangs but grew up hanging around the Logan Heights boys. My mom's best friend's sons were from that gang. Another friend of my mom had a son from the Shelltown gang. Though I was 11 at the time, they were around 19 or 20. We knew a lot of people in gangs when we were growing up. Some people think that you can't escape that when you live in the low-income areas, but there are lots of homes where peaceful people live.

My brother and I didn't have a good relationship growing up. He would bully me and beat me up a lot. To learn how to protect myself, at age 13, I joined a martial arts organization called Kajukenbo that was on the corner of Market and 14th. At that time, there was a lot of prostitution and drug dealing in that area of downtown San Diego. I went there until age 19.

During that time, I smoked a lot of sherm to help with pain when working out. I tried stopping a few times. I joined the Victory Chapel when it came out. It was a group of ex-gang members who found Christ. That didn't work out with me too long. I got to go to Hawaii for a month with them, but all I did was party; they sent me home.

I started out at Crawford High School. A lot of the blacks and Mexicans got together to fight against the Vietnamese or the Laotians.

In about 1987, I was sent to Garfield High School, a continuation school. At that time Garfield was north of El Cajon Boulevard on Oregon Street. It was pretty bad. There was a lot of gang-bang fighting.

I remember a time when a car drove up and a guy named Oso from Sherman barrio came out with a crowbar and tried to get some of the East San Diego boys. He didn't come towards me because he knew me; I'm always cool.

When I was at Garfield High, there was an auto shop teacher whose name was Mr. Yap. He was also a math teacher. When I would come into his shop drunk, he would let me sleep it off. He used to hide me and tell me how it is. He was really cool. He also let me hang out at the auto shop.

But I never graduated from high school. I went to juvenile hall many times in the late '80s and early '90s (my late teens and early twenties). Juvie was on Meadowlark Drive. I had a very good probation officer who tried to help me.

In 1997, I got my GED while I was incarcerated. I was 26. It came in the mail the next year. I just remembered the things I learned earlier and was able to pass the test. That was a period of about nine months in prison. When I got out, the US government tried to deport me, so I spent about nine months in immigration jail in Yuma, Arizona.

After my release, I was staying in Tijuana at the house which my father left me. I used some girls to transport drugs across the border. I also knew a couple of guys who were deported from Paso Robles, CA. We all ended up working together in Tijuana. We would buy meds, cocaine, and everything else really cheap in Tijuana and then have the girls smuggle them across the border. We were making a lot of money until somebody got killed.

We had everything going for us. We paid our taxes and tried not to make so much money that it would get negative attention from the big cartels. They would tax us, and we'd pay them and then the cops. We had a cool thing going until this killing happened.

One of the guys from our crew did it on his own, probably paid off by a cartel. We had not sanctioned or agreed to it. The victim got rolled up in a carpet and set on fire. Because of that, our crew split up. I ended up working in Tijuana and lying low for about four years.

It became more difficult to cross the border after 9/11. Finally, I decided it would be easier to stay in one country. I chose San Diego. I ended up selling crack on the downtown streets and doing drugs. I was hanging out in the 16th and Island area. Sometimes I would stay in hotels. For months I slept on the streets. I became a homeless street addict.

When you have everything in abundance—money, women, and drugs—you think you are OK. Without your money, you are left with horrible self-esteem, homelessness, and drug addiction.

One day I heard I could get some money by just going to school. I signed up for the Summer Summit program at San Diego City College (SDCC). I still ended up in jail for a year.

One person I met at SDCC was Auggie Sandoval of the Extended Opportunity Programs and Services (EOPS) organization. He took my phone call from jail. We figured I needed to start all over in college. He arranged to take my classes off my record so I could try it again when I got out.

Still, I was in and out of jail a few more times.

During one of the times that I was locked up, my mom found me. She came to see me with her friend Chelo. Her three sons were all from Logan. I grew up with them; they were like my brothers. One is now dead; the other two are in prison.

My mom showed me the dialysis marks on her arm and said, "My sons are killing me. Your brother is in for 27-to-life and you are all that is left. You gotta survive."

I felt bad, but when I got out of jail, I drank a little bit more.

Finally, in 2008, I went to a rehab place in Barrio Logan called *Grupo Despertar* (wakeup group). What I liked about that place was that it was so raw and non-traditional. No one is fazed with how bad or ugly your story is; you can't impress anyone at that rehab. They take you for what you are, see your positive potential, and help you achieve it.

Everyone has a sad story: "I got locked up," "My parents died," or "I didn't have a choice." But at the *Grupo Despertar* rehab, we had a saying: "No matter who dies or who is born, whatever happens, do not get high."

I graduated from there in three and a half months and never did drugs or alcohol again. That was my turning point and I never turned back.

In 2008 I started over at City College, taking classes and using the many opportunities, even jobs, which teachers and various college programs provided for me.

I used to wear all the homeboy style of clothing: gray shirts, stripes, Dickies. I started to change my way of dressing after rehab. I got rid of the cholo lifestyle. Of course, when I started taking care of myself and the way I dressed and acted, I had plenty of babes hanging around me.

Soon I met a young student named Abdulkadir Ahmed. (His brother Hashim happens to be behind me in the cover photo.) He became not only a friend but a mentor to me. Ahmed got me involved in the City College student government and many of the events on campus. In prison, everyone expected you to stick to your own race and never fraternize with people of a different race. Ahmed taught me that in the real world it doesn't matter how old you are or what your race or religion is. What matters is your discipline and maturity. I took this to heart and was always encouraging my fellow students to do their best in college. I really got that organizing experience from the street.

When you are dealing with guns, drugs, and stolen merchandise, you learn how to move people around, to influence people. Now I have traded drugs, guns, and stolen merchandise for scholarships, soliciting donations, finding and utilizing tax write-offs, and things like that.

If you are locked up and reading this book right now, you need to realize that you already have the life skills you need to succeed. We can be business majors because we have experience dealing with people. We former drug dealers can become excellent salesmen and business managers. If we can sell poison, we can sell anything. The worse we were in crime, the better we can be in the world.

If you combine this with what you believe in, you will have success. You can't just go to school or drug rehab. You have to find something that you believe in so you can give back and feel your worth and your value for your fellow citizens. You have to make peace with your past and embrace the new person that you are by challenging yourself. This is the secret.

After graduating with an AA from City College, I transferred to San Diego State University (SDSU). At both schools, I volunteered and was a student organizer with the International Students Association. Once I finished a few classes at SDSU, I learned that they have a study abroad program called the Global Village Program (GVP).

Even though I was 49 years old, far older than most of the applicants, the GVP loved my diversity of experience, especially my work at the UMI Learning Center where there are Muslim kids, grades 4 through 12, from Iraq, Syria, Afghanistan, Congo, and Somalia. Ahmed had introduced me to the UMI Center, where I also got to know the director, Mohamed Muriidi. Mohamed is very happy with my work at the center and spoke eloquently in support of my application. I got a scholarship to go to Korea with GVP for the Spring 2020 semester.

I went to Wonju, South Korea and was fine living in the dorms with 20-year-olds. The counselors had told them that I could adapt to anything. After my semester there, I was able to get my certificate of completion from the Global Peace Village at the Yonsei University. To do that, I had to mentor eight students a week for one hour each and do a cultural exchange with them. It was very rewarding. I was also able to take courses in international economics, social philosophy, and conversational Korean.

Korea is a country that has a drinking culture so, as a recovering alcoholic, I had to learn how to say, "Thank you from the bottom of my heart, but I have to refrain from drinking because I don't do that well," in Korean. I still hung out with the younger community but did not drink. In life, if you find what you believe in, you really will hard-wire yourself to stay away from drugs and alcohol because you know they're not good for you. Everyone is different.

I finished my first two AA degrees in Arts and Humanities and Politics in 2018. I am still enrolled at City College where need one business math class to finish my third, a Legal Administrative Assistant AA.

Now (February 2021), I am finishing a Bachelor of Arts (BA) in Urban Studies with a specialization in Urban Political Economy and Public Policy at San Diego State University. I expect to graduate at the end of 2021.

Right now, I am Project Specialist and Events Planner at the UMI Learning Center. The UMI center is a very important part of how I am living today. Mohamed is like a brother to me and is teaching me all about running a community center.

When you have youth that are coming from war-torn countries, they have the potential to fall into the San Diego gang subculture because they have post-traumatic-stress syndrome. They are potentially more violent than American gangs because they have seen brutality such as people being incinerated in explosions and war.

Another reason I go to UMI is to talk to the youth about drugs and alcohol. I tell them how to keep from going into gangs, forming gangs, and breaking the law. I encourage them to embrace the goodness which their parents have taught them and to resist any peer pressure to the contrary.

We also work with the parents and educate them in English and math using the Learning Upgrade software which I acquired for them. I renew it every year. I understand the parents' situation coming from a foreign country. My own mother didn't know English. It helps me to feel like I am valuable when I can help them like this. I put myself in a situation to use my skills from the past to benefit communities, preventing crime, promoting education, and so much more.

Ahmed, whom I met at City College and worked with at the UMI Center, is one of my biggest role models. He treats me like family, even inviting me to his big family reunion barbeques.

Another role model is Beto Vasquez. He is special because he has reached higher levels in the education system and has stepped into San Diego city administration posts. He was an aid to a city council person and is scheduled to finish his PhD in 2021.

Lastly, artist Salvador Torres became like a father to me. I met this community activist and internationally-known artist in 2012. He taught me the importance of helping people to find their identity and purpose.

The trick that I have learned is, "Don't be jealous of other people. Just realize that everyone has their own individual gifts to give the world." I am a living example of the fact that people can change. I shaped my own identity by watching both of those guys.

Though I have access to live in either country and go back and forth regularly, I currently choose to live in the Tijuana house which my father left to me.

I am planning to make a community center in Tijuana that will offer free English and Spanish classes that tie in with the Mexican Ministry of Public Education. People are always trying to do this kind of thing for profit. If it were free, it would really boost the atmosphere and the economic potential of the people here in Tijuana. This way, they would not have to be slaves to the maquiladoras. You can change the atmosphere of a neighborhood and change people's attitude towards corruption if you give them options to make them feel good about themselves.

There are always ways we can help people around us and improve our communities. San Diego has a program called "I Love a Clean San Diego." I have been privileged to work with them. They taught me how to organize and promote neighborhood cleanups. What a wonderful way to meet our fellow citizens. Together we can do more than we can alone. We can elicit good works from people who would like to do something good, but who never get started without some comradeship. I hope to establish "I Love a Clean Tijuana."

During the writing of this book, my brother was released in February 2021 after 27 years in prison. He was on drugs and unable to stay away from the drug culture. Just one week later, he was murdered. I found him 48 days later at the morgue. My mother died in 2013, so I have been really going through it and heartbroken. I lament my brother's loss and ask God to sustain me:

Spare me Father, do not forsake me in this life of overabundance, in this material world with no value. I feel unappreciated. Use me. I want to be used for Your greatness. Let me pay my debts to You. Let me be Your sacrifice, let me be something for You. Leave me not like this. Let me be the cause for others to not cry, to not have hunger, to not lose You like I once did. Don't let me cry alone in this world. The void of my broken heart lives in this world—yearning for a real life.

My brother had a wonderful sense of style and romance. Women would look for him. One even told me she wanted to have his baby. He was a self-starter and very intelligent. We would fight but had some great memories.

When I was in the 3rd grade at Sherman Elementary, he saved my life from a boy who wanted to stab me. While he was in prison, facing 27-to-life, he asked me to look after his son Jacob Kyle Jimenez.

I will miss him. Rest in Peace, Rafa. Now I am the only member of my family left out of my parents and two brothers. I didn't have any sisters, although my mother once told me my father had a baby girl out of wedlock and that she was in Chicago or someplace like that.

We all have different stories and go through different paths in life. My sincere hope is that one of the stories in this book will resonate with you and encourage you to change your behavior and thus change your life for the better.

5. Juan Carlos Painting, Speaking, and Campaigning

6. Artist Salvador Torres Celebrates Juan's Achievements

4 ARTHUR NIDES

I find this to be a highly interesting concept—writing about myself. I really begin by saying, "Wow, who *am* I?" Well, to begin with, I am Arthur (Art) Nides, a product of the environment and of the communities that I have been in: foster homes, youth correctional camps, jails, prisons, and several other types of institutions. All of these have impacted the shape and form of me. Though my parents cared for and loved my eight brothers and sisters and me to the best of their ability, I feel like I raised myself to get out of dire poverty.

We were a family of 11 in Covina, CA, one of approximately 80 suburbs of Los Angeles. I was born in 1960 with four older brothers and three older sisters. Then came one younger sister, so I have always been the youngest boy. That is why my parents and siblings referred to me as "baby boy."

My father, as much as I know of him, was a hard-working man who took pride in his work and in his responsibility as a father. He knew he was the foundation of the family. My parents raised us with concern and a passion for us to do what is right in life. This meant going to church and attending Catholic schools.

Though my dad worked steadily for the City of Irwindale, it was a minimum wage job. So, we were always hungry. That is part of why I started stealing things—so I could eat. I was lost in the confusion and hunger at home so, at a very young age, became institutionalized. I was made a ward of the court at age nine.

I really did not know my dad as well as I believe I should have. His drinking problem gave him ulcers and other diseases. I believe he was overwhelmed by his large family and the responsibility of caring and providing for all of us. All of that, along with his addiction, took a toll on his health and behavior. He passed away in 1973 due to his alcoholism. He was 43; I was 12.

Once my father was gone, my behavior deteriorated to even lower levels.

As a woman of Yaqui descent, my mom's beliefs and culture had only one focus: survival in this world. Indeed, her beliefs and culture were so strong that I knew I did not want to live at home once my dad passed away. It was not so much because of any disagreement with Mom, but because we had to survive and were in dire poverty. I constantly found myself never at home and always involved in something that had to do with crime and addictions. That was the only way I knew to be able to eat, buy clothes, and otherwise provide for the household.

Mom had no school education of any kind. But she had a basic instinct for the unconditional protection of her children. Not surprisingly this extended to wanting me to have an education and to follow the golden rule.

At age 16, getting my own car did not make me any more law-abiding. My mother knew that I was in a life of crime but still loved me unconditionally. I really appreciated that she accepted me as her son, no matter what I did. She did not like seeing me go to jail but supported me because I was still her "baby boy."

Before age 18, during the second nine of my formative years, I saw a long list of jails and correctional schools, including the California Youth Authority's (CYA) schools, programs, and detention camps. They concluded that I was "incorrigible." Whatever efforts there were to stem my addictions in the 1960s and '70s were ineffective.

After 18, I did time, off and on, at every state prison that most people ever heard of and a half dozen more: Soledad, Tracy, Folsom, Ironwood, and Avenal—off the top of my head. When I would get out, even when I had a job and during stints on parole, I never intended to stop using drugs.

One parole officer, who tested me in the '80s, recognized this. Though I tested dirty and fully admitted that I liked coke, crystal meth, and heroine, the official refused to violate me. A violation would have sent me back to prison for a year or so. The parole officer said, "Why bother to do that? All previous evidence indicates that you are not yet ready to surrender yourself to any kind of treatment. Why should we go to all the expense to dry you out in prison—where you'll probably get more drugs, anyway—when we know that as soon as you get out, you'll just go around the nearest corner and snort, shoot, or ingest a new dose of whatever you can find?"

I look back at my past and see that it was practically suicidal. My lifestyle in the community was a bit uncontrollable. Having spent my juvenile years in the system, I really didn't care if I was in jail or not. It was not all bad.

My mom felt comfortable knowing I was incarcerated. My brothers and sisters felt the same. They would all say, "He is safe. No need to worry; we can sleep." They knew that my safety and health were secured in jail and that I would survive.

Coming from a family where nobody ever spoke the words "I love you," hugged you, gave birthday presents, or any other indication of care or affection, I grew accustomed to, even fond of, the institutional lifestyle. The kind of love I was seeking and the care I needed was found in there.

My brothers and sisters understood this quite well. In fact, they knew I enjoyed the jail lifestyle simply because it gave me three hots and a cot, which means three meals, a warm bed, and a doctor if I needed one. I was well taken care of, so I advanced through the various levels of the incarceration hierarchy: camps, CYA, city jail, county jail, then one prison or another.

Through the decades, at the different levels I would see "regs"—the regular guys whom I had seen or known well from previous sites. Though I was never in a gang, we were friendly and exchanged homie words and various hand signals to acknowledge one another.

In 2018, I was back living in my mom's area of Covina and attending a detox site called American Recovery in Pomona. But trying to do recovery in the neighborhood I had sprung from was not working. So, my mentor recommended that I go to CRI-Help, an addiction treatment center in North Hollywood.

With their help, I now see that by going back to school, I can be an example of hope and faith to others, showing them that they just need to believe in themselves. Many people have witnessed the lifestyle I came from, all the way up to where I am now, and have told me the change is unbelievable. I am a living example that miracles can happen and of how education can increase your awareness of the value of life.

That conversion stems from my personal journey as an institutionalized drug addict to now being a college student. It took some time for me to break the jail mentality, but here I am, in college and amazed at what I am writing. It all started with the CRI-Help treatment that I finally surrendered myself to in 2018. That helped me to realize the true value of life and education.

During my time with the wonderful people at CRI-Help, I was encouraged to call my sister Terry who is 72 years old. Right before I hung up, I told her, "I love you, sister." She stated that she loved me right back. That was the first time that I ever told my older sister that I loved her.

My mom taught me that, "Friends are just people who will come and go—the only friend you will ever have is a rough one." Due to the lifestyle I had, I would see my friends turn at the drop of a hat, making trust difficult for me. However, thanks to my spiritual awakening, I am learning and discovering that not everybody has an ulterior motive in wanting to be my friend.

I still keep in touch with the homies in Irwindale who were in and out of the system before me. I looked up to them. They knew me when I was in the system and are all retired now. They are happy for me, amazed at what I am doing, and proud of how I have changed my life. I appreciate their support and now have peace of mind about my life, knowing I am doing things right.

CRI-Help has given me an open mind toward things, people, and life. They call it the concept of mindfulness. That is the constant awareness and gratitude for people, events, and opportunities in all facets of my life.

Homeboy Industries helped me tremendously. I participated in their 18-month program which included time working in the cafe but mostly attending various classes and support groups that were provided by the Educational Services Team. They pay you if you attend the classes. They go from 8 a.m. to noon for 90 days, then full-time from 9 a.m. to 4 p.m. You see a therapist or case manager, do cleaning, and go to classes. They only want your success in the education department.

They provide tutoring and give educational support to those preparing for tests like the GED, learning how to navigate community college, and using computers. Pathways to College meets every Monday with students from various colleges. Other formerly-incarcerated students who graduate take part in the program to help others follow in their path. It is almost like enjoying a childhood I never had. I feel a sense of compassion with no judgement.

On top of all that, they provide life-skills classes and groups to help those of us dealing with substance abuse and things like that. They help you to transform yourself to be able to get a job and support you in everything you need to learn to be self-sufficient and to do well in life.

You can succeed with the help of people who believe in you with sincerity and compassion, people at places like CRI-Help, Homeboy Industries, and Narcotics Anonymous (NA). I want to thank them all for the things they have shown and taught me. I especially want to thank Brittany Morton in the education department of Homeboy Industries. She and the staff and the volunteer tutors gave me amazing encouragement and inspiration in my college education.

I like the fact that I can now socialize with people from all walks of life and be non-judgmental toward those with different lifestyles. I am also happy at the fact that I am not racially biased by a long shot. That is due to the different environments I have experienced in my past. But I must admit that I can be racially biased if it is projected on me. I also believe that I can be a bit blunt with certain people whom I do profile and stereotype. I don't really care to be this kind of person with myself or anyone.

I am just now learning to be quieter and to listen more. I try not to take inventory of people so much. That is a struggle. But as our NA literature says, "One day at a time." So with the grace of God, I believe miracles can happen if people take advantage of the right opportunities—maybe not overnight, but someday soon.

I love the fact that I can acknowledge all this now. Thanks to the 12 Step Program, I seek kindness, joy, love, and happiness. In return I give those gifts freely to all. I am learning to be grateful when I wake up each morning. As Johnny Canales would say on *The Johnny Canales Show* when I was a kid, "*Essooo!*" by which he meant, "Let's begin (or end) the show."

My epiphany, my spiritual awakening, which all these previously mentioned people and agencies have given me, has led me to my new beginning at East LA College (ELAC). Don't get me wrong, I still have issues and still need a lot of tissues because the inventory of my personal defects and shortcomings leaves me with a long way to go. But I'm taking it one day at a time at ELAC. Even though I completed my 18-month program with Homeboy Industries, I still go there several times a week to get advice and support in my classes and any help I need on my laptop.

I never really felt anything positive about my educational experiences until a couple years ago. Being in the ELAC Addiction Studies class (even the parts which have been online during 2020 and 2021) has changed my life. Now I am passionate about showing people who are in poverty, gangs, addiction, and more, that higher education can truly open doors and give you a better lifestyle. At last, I strongly believe in the power of higher education. Now, at age 58, I'm a late-life convert.

My Addiction Studies program is part of the Psychology Department at ELAC under Dr. Lisa Vartanian. She heads the Chemical Dependency Program that leads to a Substance Abuse Counselor certification—and a job—helping people like me. She is a wonderful teacher and mentor. Just see the rave reviews she gets online.

As of February 2021, I am in an internship for six hours a day. They call it shadowing. That means I observe a staff member and listen to what he or she is saying in my group. There are nine or ten patients in a group with various drug or alcohol addictions.

Having been at ELAC for 18 months already, I have finished all the psychology and drug addiction coursework to become a counselor. I have a certificate: my state credential to be a counselor. Now I am doing the hands-on work to get my license.

I have my CCAPP (pronounced C-CAP) card and number from the California Consortium of Addiction Programs and Professionals (CCAPP). To get that card I did a Live Scan (finger printing and background check), took several American Society of Addiction Medicine (ASAM) online courses, and have been trained in my medical and social work Code of Ethics. The code includes things like veracity (truthfulness), social justice, nonmaleficence (doing no evil), service, competence, and the dignity and worth of all people.

The experiential internship for getting the license has two sections of practical work: out-patient (course AD 1 for 170 hours) and in-patient (AD 2 for 200 hours).

That might sound tough, but I'm already working six hours per day at L.A. CADA, which is "A Path to Recovery and Healthy Living" on East 3rd Street in Skid

Row. At that number of hours, I can knock out AD 1 in a bit over a month.

For AD 1, I'm checking people in, signing them up, and taking their temps and urine samples. There is a lot of documentation that needs to be done. The state auditors come in and check to make sure it's all being done correctly. Next week I'm going to be running my own group. I must be able to do the documentation required for that.

In addition to the internship for that ELAC class, I am taking another class in political science as well as working at my weekend job at a recovery home called Latinos on Wabash Avenue. I am constantly busy. For political science I do a lot of reading and writing up summaries in bullet points. I got an 8 out of 10 on my first exam. Sometimes I feel like a zombie, but I'm doing all the good.

Who am I? This story sums up the kind of person that I have been, have come to be, and can still become. It all stems from the communities and the environments that I have been in. I just have to learn to forgive myself. I surrender with an "amen" and an "*essooo.*" I still have time to help others. Let *The Art Nides Show* begin!

7. Arthur with Fr. Greg Boyle, S.J. at Homeboy Industries

5 JAIME MONZON

My name is Jaime Monzon. I was born at County USC General Hospital in Los Angeles on the 31st day of August 1973. My parents were both immigrants from Mexico. My father was from the state of Sinaloa and my mother from the state of Nayarit. My parents met here in California back in the early 1970s. My mother already had seven children when she met my father. I was her eighth. As a result, I have three stepsisters and four stepbrothers. Two of my brothers and one of my sisters have passed away during my life.

Being the youngest of a family of ten, I was always stuck with the hand-me-downs and the bullying from the whole family. I remember that, while growing up, all my family would get together on weekends or for special events and get drunk until they could drink no more.

My grandfather is a person who influenced me in a major way. He would often give me advice and teachings in morals and the old ways. He told me, "A man's word is a man's worth: If your word is not good, you are no good." That's why I follow through with everything I say—because of the respect and honor I feel for my grandfather. May God rest his soul. I miss him so much.

My father was another major influence in my life. He would take me back to the homeland in Sinaloa where I spent my summer and winter vacations with my father and grandfather. That's where I learned how to grow crops and take care of farm animals, including milking and feeding the cows.

My father was a very responsible and hard-working man, always providing for his family. He kept trying to put me on the right path. He paid for a couple courses to get me educated and into a career. I wasn't ready at the time. I was more into partying and using drugs. I blew my opportunities to get educated.

My father passed away in March 2018 while I was incarcerated. He is the main motivation for my schooling because that's what he always wanted for me. The loss of my father has been one of the hardest hurdles to overcome because we were very close. He was my best friend, my perfect brother, and the best dad a guy could ever have. May God rest his soul and give him the hardest hug from me up in heaven. I miss you, Dad.

I am grateful for many things that have happened in my life. I love all the good people I have met over the years. Most importantly, I am grateful to the one and only true living God for being so patient and merciful towards me and getting me away from the living hell of drug addiction and the world of drug dealers and cartels that I had grown into. I spent most of my earlier life smuggling people and drugs across the San Ysidro and

Otay Mesa border crossings. I tried to stop using drugs so many times in my life that I have lost count.

I started using drugs in the sixth grade, about 1985, with a couple of my friends by inhaling spray paint and solvents. [Editor's note: Paint sniffing was already common among the East LA homeboys in 1972.] By the time I was in seventh grade, I was smoking marijuana and selling it in the alley around the block from our home in Long Beach.

I started selling crack between seventh and eighth grade. It was the thing to do back in the neighborhood. I grew up too fast and way too soon.

My father tried to get me away from gangs and drug dealing by taking me to Tijuana and settling me there, enrolled in school. However, I found drugs a lot cheaper and easier to obtain in Tijuana, making my addiction a more severe and dangerous situation. I spent about the next 25-30 years mostly in Tijuana, until about 2015.

Although my parents lived in US, they came to Mexico on weekends and whenever they could. While I lived in Tijuana primarily, often I would try living in the states for three to four months at a time. It never worked out, so I would go back to Tijuana.

My parents never gave up on me. They always stayed close enough to monitor my activities, no matter how high and loaded I was. They would worry and cry for me when I didn't come home for a few days at a time. They would look for me at the police stations, hospitals, and even the coroner's office, thinking someone might have killed me. I put my parents through so much stress that I figure most of the health problems they had were because of me. Yet they never gave up, even when I ended up homeless on the streets. They would come around and find me.

In the latter period of my addiction, my current girlfriend would bring my parents to San Diego's skid row to help them find me. I'm grateful to my parents and to my girlfriend for not giving up on me when everyone else did.

To me, I was doing well, and my addiction wasn't a problem. According to my mindset at the time, everyone else had a problem with my addiction, but I was on top of the world.

Finally, while visiting Tijuana in October 2016, I was kidnapped by seven guys who were part of a rehabilitation crew from an organization called *Una Nueva Visión* (New Vision). They placed me by force into a rehab center for three months. That's where reality hit me. Those people gave me the tools and strength to overcome my need for drugs. They asked me to choose between a sack of dope and the love of my family, the kiss of my children, and peace of mind for my parents. That was the question that broke me. It was as simple as that.

When I got out of the TJ rehab, I went to live with my parents in Compton, CA and started working for People Ready, a temp agency. I did that for a few weeks, maybe a month or so.

Then I was hired by the Orange County Fairgrounds as a security guard during the fair because I had security experience from back in the late '90s. I worked hard and strong, making sure I was there on time every day.

That effort paid off because they kept me working at the exhibits department when the fair was over. I worked for a lady named Leslie to take down all the exhibits from around the fairgrounds. I had a lot of energy and motivation; plus, I met a lot of great people (squares according to my old mentality) and they noticed my hard work and dedication.

They kept me working until everything was taken down and put away. This is where I met Omar, the supervisor for Centennial Farms. I helped him take down all their cages and corrals as a borrowed hand from the exhibits department. That's how I got hired by Centennial Farms, one of the areas of the fairground that stays open year-round. They have everything needed to demonstrate the farming process, from growing crops to raising farm animals. They educate all of the children who visit during the fair as well as the schoolchildren who come on field trips during the rest of the year.

I worked there for about six months while living with my girlfriend in Costa Mesa, California the city of the Orange County Fair. To cut a long story short, I got into a few arguments with her. I figured that, now that I was sober, things would be easier and I would have a more trouble-free lifestyle. I ended up breaking up with my girlfriend and leaving my job. I went back home to my parents' house for a few days, but my girlfriend kept coming over, so I decided to go back to live in Tijuana.

Bad idea. Though I tried looking for work in San Diego, just across the border, I had no luck. I had a little money saved up from my previous employment, but that didn't last long. I was out of work and out of money, not the perfect ingredients for an ex-addict in TJ, the city of drug trafficking.

I started doing runs for $200-$500 for a friend of mine to Oxnard, California once or twice a month. I was eating well and spending time with my children, taking them to school and to the movies, and eating out. I was visiting my parents and doing fairly well for a short amount of time until I got pulled over at the San Onofre checkpoint between Oceanside and San Clemente. I was on my way to visit my parents in Compton because Dad was very sick.

Approaching the checkpoint, I pulled out my documents to show the officer that I was a U.S. citizen. He later said it seemed suspicious that I had my documents so readily on hand. I was sent to secondary inspection where they started harassing me about my citizenship and asked for me to open the trunk. As they were investigating me, I heard on the two-way radio that I was a wanted fugitive. The agent asked me to turn off the vehicle. I decided to flee; I put the car in gear and drove.

As I was driving away from the checkpoint, I called my parents and my ex-girlfriend to let them know that I was about to be arrested. I had a nice little conversation with them while I was doing 65-75 miles an hour—until I noticed about eight patrol cars and some civilian cars with agents in them all around me. I pulled over and said goodbye to my family.

I was dragged out of the car and handcuffed. That's how I ended up in lock-up at the Metropolitan Correctional Center (MCC) in San Diego once again in January 2018. I have a VIP membership there; most of the older staff know me from being there a few times in the past.

I worked in housekeeping at MCC while going to court off and on for 10 months. My father passed away while I was fighting my case. I was not allowed to visit him in the hospital nor to attend his funeral.

I opted for a trial since I was born in the United States of America and these were immigration agents that were harassing me about a non-existing warrant. I was so confident that I would win because I'm a citizen. But I found out that there is no winning against the federal government. They are the most corrupt and lying pieces of dirt in the whole legal and so-called justice system—that and the fact that I did run from them, LOL.

They got me for "high speed flight from a checkpoint." I also had two prior drug trafficking charges so was sentenced to five years.

I told the judge that missing my beloved father's illness and death was the hardest thing for me. "Time, I do easily," I said. "I can do the time, but now my mother is dependent on me."

The judge suspended my sentence out of consideration for the 10 months I did while awaiting hearings and sentencing. He released me on probation with supervised release, which I'm still on until 2023.

Counting the year before that MCC stint, I have now been clean for over four years and feel wonderful. I couldn't have done it without the power and mercy of God. I broke down in that TJ rehab and knelt down, asking God to free me from the burden of drug addiction.

Since getting out of prison in October 2018, I have been working at Central City Recovery run by Volunteers of America in downtown LA. I do intake and tell my story to groups as large as a dozen 3 to 5 times a week.

Thanks to my getting a DUI, I did a short program at the Southern California Alcohol and Drug Program.

A homie *veterano* there told me about courses at East LA College; I managed to get in. I have stayed focused on my schooling. I'm working toward certification as a drug addiction counselor. I chose the addictions program at ELAC because I hope to help the younger generation (especially grades 5 through 7) and all the drug addicts to make better decisions. I study subjects like experiential recovery, mindfulness, relapse prevention, and anger management.

Unfortunately, I was not able to pass classes when distance learning was mandated during the 2020 pandemic. I am waiting until in-person classes resume to finish my certificate so I can qualify for a better position. In the meantime, I am working various jobs in rehab, gaining experience. I worked for Volunteers of America, an inpatient rehab in Skid Row. I am currently working in Downey, closer to where I live, at another drug rehab place called Positive Steps that is part of Southern California Alcohol and Drug Programs.

There is a way out of the hood and out of drug addiction. There is no need to start using and end up where I did. Prison, drug dealing, and skid row are not options for people who want to better themselves and their community.

I have been getting in touch with some of my eight children. I help them out economically and spend quality time as much as my probation allows. I take them on road trips and communicate with them on a regular basis, letting them know that I am back and that if they ever need anything, they should get in touch with Dad. I will make it happen if it's within my reach. I must teach them by example now by getting the grades that I expect them to make in school. I have a goal to accomplish, and they are happy to see me getting my education.

I have been a better son to my mother, helping her out in every way I can. I bring her flowers on every payday to make up for all the troubles and worries that I gave her in the past. I learned the hard way that it's better to take flowers to a living person than to take them to a grave. My mother, my children, and my girlfriend are all very happy with the changes in my life. It really gives me the greatest feeling to know they are proud of me for my accomplishments and for being responsible with work and school.

My friends are also very happy for me and my recovery. The ones who have met me since my rehabilitation can't believe that I was a drug addict, living on skid row. My older friends have a harder time believing that I am sober because of the magnitude of my addiction back in those days. They see it and can't believe it, but it's obvious at first sight because I am 100 pounds heavier and look so much healthier now. Such friends motivate me to get good grades and to earn my money.

Some of my earlier friends come around to try to get me high; I stay away from them. I see the way their lives are going and remember where I came from. I know for sure now that I have made the right choice in my life.

My immediate goal is to be able to teach young kids in elementary, junior high, and high school how to make the right choices. My ultimate goals are to stay drug-free, finish school, and open a drug recovery site in Tijuana. Maybe I can help some of my old friends. I want to continue working so that I can be happy, make my family happy, and live a better life, a drug-free life. To everyone reading this I say, "Don't give up on your dreams, no matter how hard and unreachable they might seem."

8. Jaime as Child, at Age 20, and Circa 2021

9. Jaime Working on Resume and Job Training

6 CESAR RUIZ

I was born in Guadalajara, Mexico in 1982. When I was two years old, we came to the US. My dad was already living in East LA with some family members. Mom brought my older brother, a younger sister, and me across the bridge at Laredo, Texas. That was the border crossing closest to Guadalajara.

From Laredo, we went to East LA to meet my dad. I don't know the details of how we got there. Two more siblings were born. Later, we moved to South Central LA, and my parents split up.

I went to Lenicia B. Weemes Elementary School, a couple blocks from USC in South Central. I was not really into school but moved on to James A. Foshay Junior High School, not far from Weemes. I remember one teacher from Foshay, Miss Bibbie. She taught me either 6th or 7th grade. My daughter later had this same teacher, which is pretty cool. There were other good teachers, but Miss Bibbie was my favorite.

We had to get up early and walk to school to be there at a certain time. It was about a two-mile walk. We never had a school bus pick us up. My brother and I would meet up at school and walk home together. There was one time that some teenagers crossed the street and walked up to us. We knew they were suspicious. They pulled a gun on us and said, "Give us your money!" This kind of thing happened more than once.

We didn't always have money. Sometimes all we had were some marbles, toy cars, or Pogs. We would give them whatever we had. In the end we'd say, "Thank you," because we were so scared. Then we'd go home and tell our mom. She would say, "Thank God you just gave them whatever and they let you go. Be glad you walked away." So when it happened, we were shocked but were glad to be alive and felt blessed.

My family went to St. Odilia Catholic Church on Latham Street. I made my First Communion there. One day my family got run over by a drunk driver when we were coming out of church to the bus stop. It was my mom and us five kids. I was able to grab the oldest of my two sisters and get out of the way. My youngest sister was about a year old. Mom landed on top of her. My older brother got hit, but my younger brother was hit the worst—right in his forehead.

The injured family members were taken to the Los Angeles County General Hospital. My brother who was hit directly had to go there. Mom didn't want them to split up her kids into different hospitals, so we all went there. My brother had brain swelling and went into a coma. He spent a lot of time in the hospital, and they weren't sure he was going to make it. Fortunately, he did make it and is OK. He has a family now.

My mom did a good job raising us up until we were teenagers. We weren't troublemakers to begin with. Mom was strict with us. She had to be. Growing up like that puts you into a different state of mind.

I never dressed like a gang member. It was just poverty; we dressed in hand-me-downs. Everything was a struggle. You would get home and say to yourself, "I've had enough bullying!"

I went to high school at Manual Arts and was good at PE. I ran in cross country and did track and field. But I never graduated.

When I was around 15, I started working doing drywall with my Uncle Martin, Mom's brother. He was the closest thing I had to a father-figure at that time. It was because of him that I learned the trade that I do now. My dad was not involved during my teens.

I began my high school years hanging out with some friends and ditching school. That seemed better than going to school. I didn't know any better. The first time I got in trouble with the police happened because I got caught ditching school. By the end of 11th grade, I quit going to school.

I liked working on cars and could fix anything. That is how I earned money when I was 16, 17, and 18 years old. I would buy a car for $500, fix it up, then sell it.

I got caught by the police for driving without a license a few times. When that happened, they would take the vehicle away from me. We would have to walk home from wherever we were. One time it took us two hours to get home. That's when we were more likely to get robbed, because they would see us walking and could pull a gun on us.

When I was 17, I bought a car for myself: an '82 Firebird Trans Am. Then I could do whatever I wanted. My mom couldn't tell me no; I was driving.

I started hanging out with the wrong kind of friends. Because Mom was so strict with us, we wouldn't bring things home to her. I never joined a gang because she always put the fear in our eyes. She would say, "If you are ever going to do something, you need to do it for yourself. Don't let some other people get you involved in something you can't get out of." Still, we would go hang out with our friends doing things we weren't supposed to be doing.

Even though I was not in a gang, I would dress like that. I shaved my head and wore cholo pants—size 40—with wife-beaters. The pants were so big, we had to wear a belt that had a big initial in the buckle, like an R or a C. We wanted to blend in with everybody else.

The friends I hung out with were breaking into cars. They showed me how to do it. We used screwdrivers or whatever, even shattering the windows. I started doing those things because I wanted to be looked at as part of the group.

Then the police caught us. I remember that night. One guy wanted to break into a car; I had a gut feeling about this. I tried to say no, but he called me a pussy. It was pure peer pressure, so I went along with it and dropped him off.

After he got started, I saw a Camaro go by with two bald guys. I didn't know if they were gang members or what, but something did not look right to me about these guys. I saw them make a U-turn and come back towards us.

By then, my friend had popped the lock on the car. I yelled, "Watch it, they're coming!" He jumped into my car and the Camaro started following us. The next thing I knew, I came to a roadblock with a bunch of black and white cop cars. They had guns and a helicopter with lights there at Vermont and Figueroa. It turned out the guys in the Camaro were undercover cops.

We were taken to the police station for breaking into motor vehicles. They told everyone who was there for processing that the sergeant will ask each of us why we were there. They told the other guy and me to answer that we were there for breaking into a motor vehicle. I said, "Yes sir!"

When the sergeant came, I was first in line. He asked me why I was there. I said, "I don't know. Ask him! He's the one who brought me in here."

They said, "Wait! We told you what to say!"

I replied, "I'm not going to incriminate myself for something I didn't do. I was driving my own car." So, they separated us and interrogated us.

Finally, the other guy budged and said, "It was me that broke into it. He ain't had nothing to do with it." This guy was on probation, so he went to jail for breaking probation.

I called my mom at 5 o'clock in the morning and said, "I ain't makin' it. I'm in jail. Don't even worry about bailing me out. I'll be good. I didn't do nothing wrong. They're gonna let me go."

There was another guy there in the jail who got caught for stealing a police bike. He just got here from

Mexico and said that he went to the store to pick up some milk and saw the bike. It was still there when he came out, so he thought, "It ain't nobody's. I'm gonna take it." We asked if he couldn't see that it said Police on it. He said, "I'm from Mexico. I don't know what that means!"

Another guy across from me in the cell kept looking at me. I said, "I don't even know you. Why do you keep staring at me like that?"

He said, "Well, you look familiar."

I replied, "You don't look familiar to me so, whatever!"

That was the first time that I was really in jail and I thought, "Oh shoot! I can't just let myself be pushed around." I had spent my whole life being pushed around.

Early in the morning, my mom came and bailed me out. My older brother was there in the waiting room. He was pissed off. I caused my mom headaches spending money she didn't have. I was young and just not thinking about all of this.

After that, I tried to stay out of trouble. I had a court date coming up. At court, the judge said, "You're dismissed. There is no case against you."

I thought, "Well, I got away with this one. I might be able to get away with the next one." I kept hanging out with the same friends. We'd get caught breaking into cars, but they'd find nothing on us and let us go. We'd still hang out together.

By the time I was 19, I moved in with some friends. My mom wouldn't be happy with my friends hanging out at her place, so I would always crash at some friend's house. I wasn't working any job. Why would I? I could make a couple hundred or even a couple thousand in one night with stolen wheels or stereos or whatever was in the car.

One night, I was with a friend who was driving. Next thing we knew, there was a cop on the left at a four-way stop sign. My friend made a right and we got pulled over. We had our tools, and it had been a big night that night. I thought, "Ah hell! Here we go. We're goin' to jail again." But we got away. I felt lucky to be able to get away again.

My friend's sister would hang out with a bunch of people from a local gang. They would come over, hang out, drink, and then go home. One night they called a taxi. It was late at night. The taxi showed up.

At that time, taxi drivers sold beer after hours from coolers in the trunk. The driver jumped out and said, "How many beers do you want?"

They said, "We'll take your whole cooler!" and started robbing him and beating him up. We were just hanging out and having a good time when this thing went haywire. We heard his cries for help. When you're in the middle of it, what can you do?

My first reaction was to go snatch the taxi driver away from their hands, so I did. They looked at me as if to ask, "So what are you going to do now?" I threw the driver up against the fence, and told him, "Hey, just be quiet! Sit here and be quiet! These guys will kill you right now! You don't even know who you're dealing with."

At that point, the gang members took whatever they wanted from the driver and said, "Now you get the hell out of here."

He took off and used the taxi radio to contact headquarters. A bunch of taxi drivers swarmed the place, but by then, no one was there, so they left.

Another time, my friend's 14-year-old brother Jesse was down the street at a swap meet, hitting on some girls. The next thing you know, there were some gang members from that neighborhood chasing him back to the house. They were yelling, "We're gonna kick your ass!"

I thought, "Oh shit!" This kind of stuff happening made me realize that things were getting serious in our area.

On Memorial Day weekend, we were hanging out and it was getting late. My friend went to bed, but his little brother Jesse decided he was hungry. It was around 11 p.m. and I said, "Let's go see if the taco stand on the corner is open." We were in the front, upstairs apartment that faced the street. We went down and looked over the fence. We could see that the mobile taco stand was not there that day. I said, "Why don't I just take you to go get some McDonald's in the morning?"

We turned around and were going to go back upstairs when his friend hollered from across the street, "Hey, Jesse, Cesar!" He came over, so we stayed outside talking for a while. A car pulled up and dropped off one of the neighbors who went inside.

Another car pulled up. This one had dark windows. We were about 10 to 15 feet away. I walked a little closer, maybe 7 feet away from the car, thinking, "Who's that?" and checking it out. They didn't move or do anything. I turned around and had taken about four or five steps when I heard what sounded like firecrackers. I didn't realize at first that I was being shot at. I was so close that my ears were ringing from the noise.

I started running and yelled to Jesse, "Run!" He was right near the bottom of the steps and just froze in fear. They kept shooting. I felt like somebody pushed me; I fell.

Jesse yelled, "Cesar!" I looked up and saw Jesse get hit by gunfire. They hit him about 18 times. He went limp like a noodle and fell down.

At that point, I must have stopped breathing. I started levitating away from my body as they were shooting. I thought, "Whoa! What's goin' on?" I was up in the sky, looking down at my body. Then I came to a big movie-theater-like place and right next to me was Jesus Christ. I was amazed and felt happy to be home. He pointed to the big movie screen. It started playing my life before my eyes; all of it was true. I saw my mom carrying a little baby—it was me. Then I saw my siblings and us growing up, fighting with each other. It went to the time where I was hanging out with my friends and breaking into cars. Then it showed today where I was being shot at. Next, I saw my mom crying over my casket. I'm just watching all of this and I don't feel anything. You don't have feelings when you're gone. I was happy and thought, "I want to stay here with you, Jesus. I'm here. I don't want to go."

He said, "Look at what you are doing. You need to change your life. Look at the life you are living. Look at what's going on now. Now you're dead. A lot of good it will do for your mom. I gave you this life and I can take this life away from you, but it's not your time. I'm not calling you for now. I want you to open up your eyes and know that I am for real and the things that I can do for people."

"I just want to stay here! I don't want to leave!"

"It's not your time. I think it's time for you to go back."

The next thing I knew, I was back in my body. I got there in an instant. "Whoosh!"

The first thought that was in my head was, "You got guardian angels all over. This is not your day to go."

The next thing I did was to tell myself, "You're gonna get back in your body. You're gonna jump up and start zigzagging."

Before I knew it, I was up. They were still shooting. I was zigzagging left and right. Every time I zigged to the left, my head went to the right. Bullets came flying in slow motion. I saw them hit the concrete. It was like someone had my head and was moving it left or right while the bullets were coming toward my head.

I started running to the back alley towards the steps to the second floor. I said, "This is it!" I threw myself behind the steps, landing on some bicycles and things that were stored there. A last bullet came through the wood of the first step and hit me right in my ankle. That hurt so bad.

I came out from behind the steps. I was scared because we just got shot at. I looked around and found our buddy from across the street. He had been shot eight times. I set him up and said, "Keep calm. I'm gonna get some help." Neighbors started coming out.

Looking around, I saw Jesse lying there with blood everywhere around him. He was dead. There was no doubt about it. There were brains and stuff everywhere. I'll never forget that night.

I walked up to the neighbor lady's house and knocked hard on her door. She came out and said, "Now what the hell y'all want?" She knew us because she would sell candies, cookies, and chips at midnight.

When she opened the door, I said, "Man, we just got shot! I don't know what happened, but we got shot! You're gonna need to call the cops and the paramedics. Jesse is dead and this other guy needs help!"

As I was talking, I felt something like hot sweat coming down my back. I reached back there and touched the "sweat" and saw that I was bleeding. "Aw, shit! Oh man, I'm bleeding!" It was on my left side near my heart; I knew it was bad. I was still in shock. Now that I was back in my body, I was getting my feeling back. I then realized that when I felt like I was being pushed over, it was really that I had been shot in the back.

People started putting pressure on my wounds to stop the bleeding. The cops and paramedics showed up and took me to the hospital. I told the neighbor lady to call my mom and tell her that we got shot but that I'm OK. She told mom that I was lying in the street, so it made it worse for my mom. She rushed over there and beat me to the hospital.

I had been shot by an AK-47 at close range. The doctors told me, "I don't understand how you are alive. That bullet is lodged just inches from your heart. I don't understand why it didn't keep going and blow your heart right out of your chest. There must be a purpose for you in this life."

The investigators said the same thing. They asked, "How did you get hit only three times when Jesse got 18 hits?"

I was shot in my back by the left shoulder blade, in my ankle, and in the back of my calf.

There were two guys doing the shooting. One had an AK-47, and the other had a .22 rifle. Jesse's brother woke up and had just come out of the upstairs door when it all started. He saw everything from upstairs, but they didn't see him way up there. He said that they both were wearing trench coats and pulled out the guns. I never found out who they were. The police called it a late-night drive-by shooting.

I was at Martin Luther King hospital because I didn't have any insurance. We called it "King Killer." They didn't take much care of me. I was bleeding in the same bedding for days. They didn't change my bedpan. I couldn't move at all. I was handicapped. The only thing I could move was my right hand so that I could hold onto the bar at the top of my bed. That was it. I couldn't walk. I couldn't clean my butt. I couldn't do nothing. I was critically injured. I had shrapnel in my eye that they had to take out with surgery that required peeling my eyelid back.

My mom, my aunt, and a couple of my old friends visited me in the hospital. With all the friends I had, I thought, "Where are they at?" Not one of the guys I hung out with, breaking into cars, came to visit me. "Where's all my stuff?" They all took off with it. They thought it was strange that the other guy got killed and not me.

The bullet in my ankle came out by itself; my body rejected it. I still have the one in the back of my calf. I can still feel it. That one is a .22 bullet. The bullet that hit my back is an AK-47 bullet and is still lodged in there to this day. It's right behind my heart and has scar tissue over it. I also have shrapnel in my head, my legs, and all over my body. The doctor said that if any of it had hit the main bloodstream, I could have died from it.

I always have back problems because of that AK-47 bullet. When it is cold, it feels like a piece of ice. It burns kind of like an ice cube does in your mouth when you feel like you gotta take it out. But they can't take the bullet out; I just have to deal with the burning feeling. Nerves radiate the feeling to my arm, my chest, and my back.

There were three of us who were shot that night: Jesse, his neighbor buddy, and me. There were three different outcomes. Jesse died, the neighbor was hardened, and I was changed for the better. The neighbor buddy became like a rebel with an attitude like, "I don't give a shit!" He started carrying a gun and getting into gang activity.

I see it as the blessing God gave me—that of the three options, I was given the best one. He gave me a second chance to be able to change my life and to open my eyes and say, "There is a God who makes and takes your life." I'm glad He gave me my second chance. Jesse was not as lucky as I was. He was just 14. I had just turned 20. I would have given my life for Jesse if I could have. I believe it was meant to be; God had already planned the way it was going to go down. He chose me and not Jesse and I don't know why. This really humbles me.

After I got out of the hospital, I spent two months in a wheelchair. I tried to rehabilitate myself because I couldn't afford a doctor. After a while, there were rumors going around. They were trying to figure out if I was behind the shooting since I didn't get killed. My mom believed the rumors and said, "I need you to leave. I don't care where you go. Just leave. I'd rather talk to you long distance than to never see you again, six feet under the ground."

I had an African American friend at the time who was going to go to Jackson, Mississippi. He knew what I was going through and said, "I'm going to visit my brother in Jackson, Mississippi. You want to go? Let's get you out of here."

I said, "Sure! Hell, let's go!" We caught a Greyhound bus to Jackson. The only thing I had with me was a little backpack with one or two changes of clothes. That was it. I didn't have any money or anything. I was able to get the money for the bus from my mom and some friends. We stayed there in Mississippi for a while, but like everything, it grows old.

He said, "I'm going back to California. What are you going to do? Are you going to get a ticket?"

"I ain't got no money. I ain't workin'. I don't know nobody I can get money from."

So, I asked my dad, who was living at the time in Fort Smith, Arkansas. I called him and said, "Hey, I'm here in Jackson, Mississippi and I would like to come over there. I'm already here, so why the hell go back to California?"

He said, "I'll come and get you." It was about six or seven hours away by car. He came and picked me up. I stayed with him for a while. I did a little work in drywall. That was the only trade I knew and that I learned from my uncle as a teen in LA.

After a while, I moved to a small town in Arkansas. I earned some money and learned how to be an adult, paying my bills and things. I had my own company for seven or eight years. I'm now working for a heating and air company, learning a new trade. I have three boys in Arkansas and two kids back in California that are with their mother.

Since my experience when I was shot, I hear the Lord telling me, "You gotta tell people what I did for you and how I spared your life." I have given my testimony in church. I now know that God is real and that there is no other way. No matter what you do, He will still forgive you and love you. He was the only perfect man and was crucified for our sins. To this day, I'm not afraid of dying. I know what it feels like.

After all these years, many people have forgotten about me. But I am so happy to have been able to straighten out my life after growing up in the ghetto, to be a family man, to be hiring people in my own company. It made me a better, humble person, someone who wants to help other people, who sees someone in need and thinks, "That could be my kid," or, "That could be my family." My life is a blessing and I hope someone else will be blessed by reading my story.

7 STEVEN GONZALES

I first met Linda Merchain in 1976 when I was just six years old and she was still known as Miss Linda Lamkin. I was starting first grade in Room 13 at Garfield Elementary School in Alhambra, CA. The first thing I noticed when entering the classroom was a menagerie of small animals. The overall atmosphere seemed wholesome and very oriented toward learning.

Unfortunately, that first day would be the beginning of a long and troubled life filled with poor decisions, misbehavior, and ultimately acts of increasing criminal sophistication and violence.

Ms. Lamkin, as I have called her for most of our relationship, has told me time and again that she saw something special in me that first day and that, because of this insight, she knew our lives would be forever interrelated. Unbeknownst to me, on that first day I would commit one act that would become the foundation of a lifelong connection.

What compelled me to carry out this act, I will never know. Shortly after the start of class, I simply got up and walked out of the classroom, planning to never return. I stopped at a short retaining wall down the street and sat down.

Soon a car pulled up and Ms. Lamkin emerged. I could not understand why she was there, though I was pleased to see her; she was and still is very pretty. Ms. Lamkin approached, sat down next to me, and engaged me in conversation. Years of drug abuse and other difficulties have deteriorated many of my early memories, so I cannot recall the exact nature of our conversation. It must have had a significant impact on me because I did return to school with her.

Nevertheless, the two years spent in her classroom were fraught with a lot of disturbing and disruptive behavior on my part. Even so, I received tolerance, patience, and compassion from Ms. Lamkin and her aides. As much as I wanted to, I was unable to conduct myself in any manner that was acceptable. As a result, I failed to form positive social bonds and to progress at the proper academic level. It was not that I fell behind. I simply had no interest in doing the work and, as Ms. Lamkin has admitted, it appeared that I was simply bored.

Instead of reporting my misbehavior to the principal where I would suffer corporal punishment, Ms. Lamkin used a wonderful teaching tool: She required disruptive students to copy a page out of the dictionary. The goal was to improve the fine motor skills necessary for penmanship. What neither she nor I anticipated was that, for me, there was something genuinely soothing, engaging, and intimate about copying words from one page to another. This quickly became the cause of my misbehavior rather than the effect.

Astute Ms. Lamkin didn't take long to recognize this. She said, "If you want to copy dictionary pages, that's fine. No need to act out just to *earn* that privilege." My behavior improved, but not as much as my fascination with words and language.

By second grade I had grasped language in ways uncharacteristic of a seven-year-old. Because of this and my obvious behavioral issues, Ms. Lamkin explained my unique aptitudes to my parents and encouraged them to explore nurturing my talents. To stave off an obviously increasing incorrigibility and potential delinquency, my parents and the school district took action.

As early as third grade I was put into a creative writing class. At first it was a lot of grammar and sentence construction lessons, but eventually we began to start writing and reading a lot. I loved the writing exercises but hated the reading, especially the classics. We were being exposed to a variety of literature in my writing workshop. Then one day, we were given some poems to study. That was it; I was home.

One of the first poems that I can recall reading was Emily Dickinson's "Because I Could Not Stop for Death." I simply fell in love with it. What struck me so profoundly was that in poetry there was a beautiful freedom. Words could and often did come together to form a picture of the world around us, one in which I could take refuge from my years of inner childhood pain. I found my voice in a medium that speaks to those with ears discerning enough to hear the music. I began to create interesting and unique works.

When I was placed into my first creative writing workshop, my mother, who was and still is a voracious reader, believed that once I had honed my writing skills, I would likely become some great, successful novelist. My stepfather was at least content to believe that, although writing was not a viable way to earn a living, if I did become good enough, I might be able to earn a meager living. So, they continued to support my creative writing.

By about the fourth or fifth grade, I knew that I wanted to focus my writing exclusively on poetry. One day I made the bold decision to share this with my parents. Though they had been marginally supportive by paying for my lessons, the revelation that I wanted to become a poet would lead to a tremendous amount of rejection, isolation, and distress for years to come.

For my mother, the decision was just one more disappointment. My stepdad had a far more hostile view. He believed that poetry is for faggots and sissies and that if I decided to write poetry, I would be a faggot and be unwelcome in his house. He berated me, challenged my sexuality, and vociferously professed that he would never support a poetry-loving, queer son and that any time he caught me writing poetry, he would beat my ass.

I prudently took painful efforts to conceal my poetry, often writing in secret and hiding my writing implements from my parents. It felt like I was doing something sinful or perverted, yet incredible and exciting. Despite all the resistance and contempt my parents showed, they continued to allow me to attend creative writing sessions.

The struggles and emotional conflict of my home life were compounded by the anxiety that came with a new writing instructor. In traditional and classical poetry, form and meter are necessary elements. This was not lost on me. I explored every form of verse, memorized all the metrical units and line lengths, and could accurately write and scan both qualitative and quantitative verse. But this new instructor was tyrannical and unforgiving in her tutelage, expecting perfection and flawlessness.

On more occasions than I care to recall, a piece I turned in was rendered non-existent and discarded in the trash where I was forced to leave it, simply because I may have permitted an acute accent to play where a grave accent should have been found or curtailed a line or employed enjambment to give the poem more melody or depth. At these times she would harshly admonish us students that any deviation from the appropriate form was unacceptable. She would often confiscate the piece because it was flawed and therefore should not and could not exist as a poem. For me, this was devastating because I had developed an intimacy with the words that I bore to the world and the letters I wove into the fabric of my own essence.

I could easily write precise forms, placing every accent where it belonged and putting every meter in place. But soon I felt I had to sacrifice inspiration and creativity for rigid structure, uncompromised form, and the strictness of order, all of which now seems to have contributed to my problems.

For my writing teacher, reality required all things to be in their determined place; unless this condition was maintained with absolute dedication, the entire universe would effectively fall apart. For me, if the beauty of a poem were rendered non-existent simply for lacking a determined metrical unit, then surely reality could be disrupted if all things were not in their place.

I spent my elementary school years becoming an increasingly disruptive delinquent as well as struggling with conflicts in writing. I began to resent writing. I continued to get in trouble in school, even having some minor run-ins with the law.

I was a terror to students and a cancer to the teachers at Garfield Elementary; I refused to do the schoolwork. This, however, proved beneficial on two fronts. First, my regular suspensions meant less disruption of classes. Secondly, for me it meant being excused from doing schoolwork yet being passed to each subsequent grade as long as I could perform satisfactorily on assessment tests.

Through all of this, I continued to pay visits to Ms. Lamkin and was received with the utmost kindness and acceptance.

Our family home was across the street from the school. For this reason, we kids took advantage of the proximity and regularly utilized the school as our own personal amusement park. We would often spend entire days within the seclusion of the chain link fences.

During summer breaks, we climbed on the roofs, built pyramids with the outdoor lunch benches, and raced our bikes all around the school property. One summer day, as we were riding our bikes, we rode past Room 13 and noticed that a strange man was alone inside the classroom that belonged to our beloved Ms. Lamkin.

We were small children, maybe 10 or 12 years old, but we knew then and there that this man should not get away with violating that special classroom. As we crept up to the classroom, I told my younger brother to go across the street to the teacher's aide's house and to tell him to call the police. As my brother did so, a friend of mine and I kept vigil on the intruder. The man detected us and ran from the classroom.

As we gave chase, thankfully the man did not turn on us; we were surely no match for a full-grown man. He got away. Subsequently the security patrol company sent one of their guards to investigate. Ms. Lamkin was contacted to report to her classroom to see if anything was missing.

Rick Cavasos was the security guard who responded. Little did we know that Linda's encounter with him would ignite the spark that would lead to two wonderful human beings finding the love of their lives which would result in the beginning of an extraordinary union and the creation of new generations of beautiful human beings.

From what I have been told by Ms. Lamkin (hereinafter to be called "Linda"), she knew immediately that Rick was the man for her. They married sometime shortly after that first encounter and, during the next several years, brought into this world three beautiful baby girls, who have all gone on to be successful women and to start families of their own.

Unfortunately, before Rick could take part in the joyous occasions of seeing his daughters married, he contracted lung cancer and passed away. Linda lost her husband and the father of their children. After some time, Linda was able to discover love again. She married Ray Merchain, a wonderful man and the one whom she readily admits was her one, true soulmate. Sadly, Ray passed away years later, also from cancer.

I continued to stay in touch with Linda.

As I began seventh grade, my understanding of reality was turned upside-down. A new creative writing instructor took over. This man was the extreme opposite of the woman from whom I had taken instruction for the past four years.

It was at this time that I was introduced to contemporary writing, with an emphasis on free verse, cubist poetry, and the Beat Generation of writers. I remember one of the first things the man said, "Everything you have learned, all the forms, metrics, and structures you have mastered and committed to memory, are no longer relevant or necessary. Truly creative writing is not confined by rules and structure. It is free, unkempt and chaotic."

Jarring though this was, it initially appealed to me because I had become increasingly anxious when writing, fearful that any deformity would mean the end of my poem. This intellectual upheaval just amplified my evolving, anti-social attitudes and my defiance, rejection, and distrust of rules, structure, and laws. New freedom was a refreshing departure from years of emotional and creative imprisonment; however, it fertilized and sprouted seeds of psychological damage that would drive me for the next forty years.

I was able to internalize the concepts of the Beat poets and found a weak voice for my free, open, and unstructured poetry, while covertly incorporating traditional form and meter. I also applied Beat concepts to abstract constructs. Yet eventually I lost my passion and was more tortured than thrilled by my art.

As I grew more delinquent and anti-social, I also slipped away from the creativity that once gave my life meaning. Poetry became almost an enemy and, though I continued to write periodically, I essentially quit crafting poetry.

In 1984, my mother made the decision to move to the Central Valley of California, to Bakersfield. At 14 years of age, I was not happy about such a move. On the night I was supposed to go with my mother to Bakersfield to register for high school, my younger brother volunteered to go in my place so that I could stay another night with my friends and girlfriend.

That became a disastrous decision, for, on that night, I committed auto theft and burglary. I was sentenced to a juvenile probation camp. While in camp my family completed the move to Bakersfield. Upon my release six months later, I found myself living in a new and strange place. I was distraught. I tried to adapt but found it to be such an alien environment that I kept escaping to Alhambra.

Each time, of course, I visited Linda. I always felt welcome as she boasted to her students that I had been one of her best students—an utter misrepresentation contrived out of her extraordinarily affectionate nature. I loved visiting her and her classroom.

In 1985, I led a high-speed police chase. On my motorcycle, I collided with a barricade on a dead-end street. That put me into a hospital for several months. Once released, I returned to Bakersfield, and was soon thereafter committed to the California Youth Authority (CYA) for a lengthy term of incarceration.

When I was released in 1989, I went back to Alhambra to visit Linda in Room 13. She received me with the same incredible support, introducing me as one of her best students. This was the last time that I saw Linda until she visited me in prison, approximately nine years later.

After my release from CYA, I did make a half-hearted attempt to function as a working, law-abiding person and managed to do so for almost a year. My natural inclination to reckless behavior, however, soon prompted me to visit friends for whom criminal activity was the norm. I mainly engaged in drug dealing and substance abuse while doing short stints working with methamphetamine cooks. Once my "employment" with the cooks ended, I was truly back in the throes of full-fledged criminal activity. I had rekindled my love affair with weapons, especially firearms, and reverted to using violence as my primary means of resolving problems.

For the five years after my motorcycle crash, I had been involved with a girl. This relationship was the epitome of dysfunction, co-dependence, enabling, and emotional/psychological abuse. Nonetheless, we were engaged.

One day in early 1991, I went with my uncle to deliver meth to some girls in a hotel room. When we arrived, I was immediately struck by the beauty of one of those girls and decided that she and I were meant to be together. I soon learned that she had the same conviction.

We began to see each other frequently and ended up securing a place together in a nice little townhouse. The problem was, I was still engaged.

The solution was a no-brainer. I broke the engagement.

Now there were newer and bigger problems. My beauty loved it when I was a bad boy; so I made sure to be the "baddest" boy she could ever know.

I romanticized our relationship as a Bonnie and Clyde connection and began to involve her in my criminal activity, such as dealing drugs, carrying guns, and being a general menace to others in the sub-culture to which we belonged.

This escalated to committing armed robberies, car jackings, and violent attacks against others. My girlfriend encouraged this behavior, making my criminal and violent acts the catalyst for erotic intimacy.

It was not enough. Soon she began to accompany me on some of those excursions. At that time, my ex-fiancé's younger brother needed a place to stay, having burned many bridges in his personal life due to substance abuse and his own criminal behaviors. I thought it would be beneficial to take him on as a partner. The three of us spent the next six months terrorizing our community and treating life, freedom, and others as inconsequential. We became a plague on society.

In late 1991 and early 1992, the three of us brought our criminal careers to a pinnacle. Within a period of just over two weeks, we committed a string of armed robberies, kidnappings, and home-invasion robberies that culminated in the crime of premeditated, attempted murder for which I was sentenced to prison for "life with the possibility of parole plus twenty-three years."

I would rather not go into the details of these crimes; I have no desire to sensationalize my horrible behavior. Suffice it to say that after much retrospection, it is very clear to me why society felt the need to, as the adage goes, "lock me up and throw away the key."

Once in prison my behaviors continued to be abhorrent. I embraced every aspect of my violent persona with no intention of changing. In the 1990s and through the 2000s, a life sentence really meant for life, so I had no reason to change. I was resigned to the fact that I would be in prison for the rest of my life. I was certainly going to make it as difficult for prison officials as I anticipated it would be for me.

When my mother visited me in 1997, I was at Salinas Valley State Prison in Soledad, CA. She informed me that she had run into Linda at a grocery store in the Los Angeles area. Linda had asked if I might mind corresponding with her; of course, I had no objection. Several months passed before my mother gave Linda the address, but when she did, it was not long before I received a letter from Linda. I wrote back immediately, honestly answering her questions and sharing with her what had transpired in my life since last seeing her in 1989—how I had failed so terribly that society felt it was necessary to place me in prison for life. In her next letter, there was no judgment, no contempt, nor any disappointment for how my life had turned out, only caring and love and an extension of friendship through correspondence for as long as I wished it. This was the start of a new phase in a friendship that has now surpassed 40 years.

I think it was 1998 when Linda visited me for the first time in prison—Salinas Valley State Prison. Since that first visit, Linda has visited me several times in different prison locations.

In 2007 or early 2008, while I was at the Substance Abuse Treatment Facility and State Prison in Corcoran, CA, Linda came to visit me. By then, I had already been housed on the Sensitive Needs Yard for several years because of my disassociation from prison gangs (that's another story).

During that visit, I shared with Linda how I had discovered that the California Department of Corrections and Rehabilitation (CDCR) offered opportunities for prisoners to get college degrees. They only had to pay for the cost of books. I explained that my mother had promised to provide the funds so that I could begin a community college program. As an educator herself and one who had always felt that I had the capacity to excel in academics if I applied myself, Linda was naturally enthusiastic and encouraging. I felt a great sense of self-worth with the belief that I would be finally participating in a formal educational endeavor, especially when facing the reality that I was a ninth-grade drop-out who only received a GED while in the CYA. I could see in Linda's eyes that my decision was one that she was proud of.

Months went by and my mother failed to follow through on her promise, something I was accustomed to. I was not able to begin college. Linda came to visit again. She inquired whether my mother had provided the resources necessary for me to begin college. The answer was no.

Linda seemed saddened, appeared to be in deep thought for a moment, and without any indication of what was to come, said the words that I will never forget for as long as I live: "If you really want to go to school, I'll pay for it for you, for as far as you want to go."

I was floored, but my initial reaction was to politely decline. As badly as I wanted to accept, I simply felt that it would be inappropriate to do so. I mean, how could I accept such a generous offer from someone who has a growing family to provide for, who is not biologically related to me, who honestly owes me nothing, and whom I could likely never repay?

No, I certainly could not accept her offer. As politely as I was able, I declined. The remainder of her visit was pleasant and filled with normal conversations about what we have been doing, how our families are, and the like. She didn't bring the matter of college up again, nor did I.

When I returned to my facility after the visit, I shared with a few of my friends that Linda had offered to pay for my college and that I had declined because I felt too prideful. Every single guy said the same thing: I was being stupid; if Linda wanted to do it, I should agree.

At Linda's next visit, I did accept. She had no doubt that I would succeed and reiterated that she would help me go as far as I wanted.

In summer 2008, almost 20 years since Linda's first prison visit, I enrolled by mail at Coastline Community College (CCC), taking counseling and biology. At the end of that session, when I received my grades, a B and a C respectively, I seriously considered quitting college. I told Linda about my grades and about my doubt whether I was suited for college. It was then that she taught me one of the most important lessons in my academic career. She asked me, "First, did you try your best?"

I answered, "Yes."

Then, "Did you pass the class?"

"Yes."

Finally, the one question that still guides me, "Did you learn anything from the courses?" It took only a moment to realize that I had in fact learned a considerable amount and had retained much of it.

I responded, "Yes." Linda then explained that I shouldn't focus too much on my grades, but just do my best. Naturally, I should try to pass the classes, but it was more important to learn as much as possible. That has helped me to avoid the anxiety and self-doubt which I experienced in that first summer session. Subsequently, I have earned As and Bs.

After the summer of 2009, the prison canceled the college program and did not resume it until fall 2011. I immediately registered and in 2012 I completed my Associate of Arts (AA) degree in Social and Behavioral Science.

The prison held its first graduation in years for those having earned their General Educational Development (GED) certificates. Because I had earned an AA degree, I was asked to give the graduating class an inspirational speech. The graduates could invite guests to the graduation if they were approved visitors.

I naturally invited Linda. Writing my speech, I deliberately mentioned her inspiration and assistance. When giving it, I was barely able to restrain my tears. Linda didn't even try. She was soaked in tears. For decades I had caused many people to cry, especially loved ones, but for the first time in my life, I was the source of tears of absolute joy. I will never forget how this emotion felt; nor will I stop trying to duplicate it by my future actions.

After the graduation, Linda asked, "What do you plan to do next?"

My mind was foggy, but she was as focused as always. She suggested, "Find a university and start the registration."

It took time, but in 2014, I found a university in Santa Ana, CA which offers a Bachelor of Science degree entirely through mail correspondence. California Coast University (CCU) is nationally accredited and backed by several agencies that verify accreditation. In any one semester it has approximately 8,000 students enrolled. I let Linda know that I had found a school, sent her the application information including the cost, which was $9,450, and held my breath.

I thought, "There's no way Linda is going to pay that kind of money." Nonetheless, the next letter I received was from CCU, welcoming me to their institution and giving me my CCU student ID number. I was officially an enrolled undergraduate in a Bachelor of Science program in psychology.

I took to my new studies like a duck to water with my newfound love of learning. I quickly realized that this might be a route to my release. I intend to pursue a career in gerontology and an undergraduate degree in psychology would be a logical foundation for that.

CCU accepted 63 transfer units (about 21 courses) from my AA, and that meant that I needed to complete another 63 units, mostly in my core requirements. There were 11 psychology courses in a variety of disciplines; I thoroughly enjoyed each one. I was also fortunate enough to take courses in criminal justice and health care administration, which are both subjects that are and will be relevant in my life.

My initial goal was to have my BS finished within two to three years, but systemic obstacles put in place by the CDCR, primarily by the education department, delayed that time frame. Nonetheless, I was determined to finish this program and make Linda proud. For the first time in my life, I was able to achieve a 4.0 grade point average (GPA) for a 12-unit semester.

The year 2018 was a trying one for my academic endeavors. The prison had been inconsistent with the distribution of books. The education department seemed to be impeding access to higher education programs. With only four classes left to complete my BS, it seemed like nothing was going in my favor. At one point I even attempted to complete one of my classes without having received the necessary textbook. I thought that because of my background in writing, a lower division English class would be a breeze—an arrogance that would later cost me. Nevertheless, if anything, I am resilient and persistent. In late 2018, I received the textbook for my very last class.

I immersed myself, was able to complete it in just four weeks, requested the final exam, and within six weeks had finished that last class and completed all the courses required to fulfill my academic obligations.

There was still the matter of the outstanding financial obligation—several thousands of dollars.

Any anxiety was unwarranted. I discovered that Linda had already paid. All I needed to do was to submit my petition for graduation. I was so grateful.

I had not only finished the degree but was going to have it in hand before my next Board of Parole Hearing (BPH). This was something that I felt was going to be necessary and beneficial to be found suitable at the BPH.

On June 12, 2019, I received my Bachelor of Science degree in psychology, on which was also printed "Magna Cum Laude." I had graduated "with great praise," having completed my program with a GPA of 3.71. The document came in a magnificent navy-blue portfolio with "California Coast University" imprinted on the front in gold lettering. The inside of the front cover of the portfolio was lined in a textured, red satin.

The degree itself, printed ornately on parchment paper, was fixed under a clear sheet of plastic, held in by red-satin corner pieces. The degree was printed in black Old English lettering, except for the C-C-U initials of the university name across the top. Those were raised, silver letters with metallic, red-and-gold-shadow highlights.

The university seal was at bottom-center of the degree in raised, metallic gold with red highlights. The document was signed by the president of the university, the vice president of student affairs, and the dean of the School of Behavioral Sciences.

I have never possessed a more incredible item in my life, and when I received it and saw the document for the first time, I cried. What I had in my hands I knew I had earned. What it signified could never be taken away from me.

In the speech that I presented to my AA graduating class in 2012, I said that the most important things we learn from school are not necessarily the technical materials presented through each class, but the understanding of humanity that we gain from being exposed to a wonderful, cultural diversity in a myriad of subjects that allows us to view the world through a multitude of lenses.

I have told Linda repeatedly that her blessing of putting me through school has saved my life. I do not make this claim lightly. One might ask how something as simple as helping a person get through school could effectively save his life. I can say in all earnestness that, for one who has scorned education for decades and is now taking advantage of his opportunities to realize his potential, what Linda has done means everything.

Despite my belief that a bachelor's degree would benefit me at my next BPH hearing, not a single eye even batted at my academic achievements when I appeared before the BPH. In fact, prior to my hearing, my correctional counselor informed me that the BPH had advised me to "upgrade educationally," as though three AA degrees and one BS degree were insignificant. Even though there is empirical evidence that for each successive degree a prisoner earns, his or her recidivism rate is exponentially reduced, my accomplishments meant nothing. The hearing proved that the rhetoric CDCR regurgitates to the public about the promotion of education and the value and necessity of prisoners furthering their education, was mere chatter.

There are 17 BPH Commissioners statewide. My hearing was conducted by only two. They denied my parole for up to three years based on their interpretation of something I said or did during my interview. They perceived that I lacked internalization of the core concepts of my self-help programming and my college course work. That now includes, not only my degrees, but completion of 50 prison self-help groups and my having written a self-help workbook which the CDCR has used to some extent.

I find solace in the fact that one year from the date of the hearing in October 2020, I will likely receive another hearing because of new legislation.

Since being in prison, I decided that I can succeed in academics despite all prior indicators to the contrary. Because Linda believes in me now, just as she did when she punished me 44 years ago by giving me a dictionary page to copy, I have found some success.

For 44 years I have been infatuated with words, language, and the magic which can be created through the alchemy of alphabets and human emotion. I kept a journal for most of my turbulent youth and penned hundreds of poems and a dozen essays before the traumatic drama of my infant twenties. All these have been lost due to relocations, incarcerations, theft, and destruction by others, mainly because no one could understand the significance of my work to me and to the psychological world.

For twenty years I quit journaling and only returned to it in 2015. That activity is highly underrated today. It has not only taught me to write, to think life through, to see the beauty of life even in its darkest moments, but the discipline alone opens infinite possibilities and leaves a legacy, if not for the literary world, at least for those who love me and for my progeny.

Think of all your relatives and ancestors about whom you know absolutely nothing except a name you may have heard or have seen on a family tree. Only humans have the capability of leaving records to tell their great-great-grandchildren what they did or aspired to do, but fell short of and why. Most of us learn, sooner or later, from our mistakes. The lessons we leave may help our nieces or nephews.

I currently have a collection of 454 original poems, a few essays, and one unfinished long poem of approximately 2500 lines. I am a participant in the Playwrights Project, Out of the Yard Program sponsored by the William James Association Prison Arts Project, the California Arts Council, the Commission for Arts and Culture, and the Sidney E. Frank Foundation. Two scripts have been performed by San Diego State University theatre students. I am co-author of a self-help workbook used by the Mental Health Department here at Donovan State Prison.

As the spirit moves, I am also a student of Spanish, French, Latin, and Greek.

No matter what comes from here on out, I know that Linda will always believe in my potential. That belief has been so ingrained in me that it will continue to motivate and encourage me.

Linda alluded to the fact that my university offers master's degree programs. After confirmation of her continued support, I submitted my application to begin master's studies in psychology and received my first coursework in February of 2021. I hope to complete this degree by early 2022.

I would like to conclude by reflecting on something I once read. When Michelangelo was asked how he was able to create such beautiful works from crude and raw blocks of stone, he is said to have replied, "I saw the angel inside and I carved until I set it free."

That same attitude suffused a gifted teacher one autumn day in 1976 when a young, raw, and forlorn slate of squirmy humankind was put into the hands of one of humanity's greatest artists. For the next 44 years she hammered, chipped, chiseled, and carved until what she could see inside an unruly disaster of a boy, had been set free.

The world is blessed by Linda and all teachers like her. I will be forever indebted to Linda for her selflessness, compassion, and for her constant presence in my life. She has given me the gift of becoming who I am today—finally a man.

10. Steven at Age 14 and in Prison at 23 and 49

11. Steven At Donovan Prison Circa 2021

8 GILBERT GODINEZ

I was born in Montebello in Beverly hospital in January 1967. We lived in Montebello for the first five to six years of my life. Then we moved to the City Terrace neighborhood of East LA. Our house in Montebello had to be torn down so they could widen Montebello Boulevard. I still remember the address: 403 S. Montebello Blvd. It was a big change to move to East LA, which was more of a gang environment.

Every Beverly Hills needs its East LA. Somebody needs to clean their houses, cut their grass, and raise their kids. One senator told me that when a law is proposed that benefits the rich, half of East LA is on parole, so they can't vote. A quarter of East LA is too tired, so only a quarter is left to vote against the law, and it passes.

Since my older siblings were already in junior high and high school in Montebello, they were allowed to continue their schooling there. I was starting kindergarten, but we all went to school in Montebello even though it was five miles away.

When my dad would go to jail, it was back to potatoes and weenies every day. My dad would drink, get angry, and hit my mom. Some of my earliest memories are of my mom being knocked out. When things were good, it was good, but when it was bad, it was bad.

We would escape to my nana's house. She had thirty-six grandchildren, so Nana's house was the place to be. Hers was right next door to our house that was torn down. It was right next to the railroad tracks. My mom had eight sisters so there was the equivalent of a whole schoolroom full of grandkids.

I liked school and wanted to do my best, but it seemed like I couldn't grasp some of the material. I was always afraid to ask questions. I later learned that there are three types of learners: auditory, visual, and tactile. I took a test and found that I am a balance of all three. Anyway, I did well up through the eighth grade.

In ninth grade, I smoked my first joint after school. It was homegrown weed and there were nine of us who smoked that one joint. Everyone said, "I'm buzzed! I'm buzzed!" We didn't even know what a buzz was.

In high school my first vehicle was a moped. I let my hair grow long to get the stoner-rocker status.

In tenth grade, I was going against the grain. We broke the vice-president's windshield because he was always picking on us. He fixed it by lunchtime, and we broke it again.

I got thrown out of Montebello High School and then went to Vail High School. It was an alternative high school that was more like a party school, at least back then. Everything was sex, drugs, and rock and roll. Cocaine was prevalent. This was before Reagan's anti-drug campaign with the slogan "Just Say No." TV shows like *Chico and the Man*, *Sanford and Son* and *The Huxtables* all had family and career-oriented themes.

When I was sixteen, I drove a Volkswagen and my nineteen-year-old brother drove a motorcycle. He had girls, and there were parties everywhere. Then he passed away from a motorcycle accident. They checked his concentration levels; he wasn't high. His death was a shock to the family. My mom and dad both started drinking. Even the dog was upset because he knew something was missing at the house.

Juvenile hall was one of the best learning experiences of my life. I learned from the probation officer as well as my dad who was a type of "jailhouse lawyer." He learned about legal stuff whenever he was in jail.

After a few months, I was due to appear before the judge for sentencing. They wanted to give me two years. Instead, I got probation. I used things my dad had taught me and wrote up my defense. I went right up and gave it to the judge who read it. It was the same thing that I told the probation officer: that I just went the wrong way because of my brother's death.

After my brother's death, the family had spread out. One brother went to Sacramento to live with my older brother. My sister was married and had a three-year-old daughter. They were living a good life up in Paso Robles like *Little House on the Prairie*. She was pregnant with a boy and wanted me to come live with them. She told me she would pick me up from juvenile hall.

They let me out on probation in my sister's custody. I thought, "Hey, I'm alright. I'm good." I didn't think I needed to go with her to Paso Robles. I just wanted to go back to the streets for girls and drugs, so I stayed in LA. I have regretted this decision ever since. It broke her heart.

Then she delivered her baby. In the hospital, she contracted a rare, one-in-a-million virus. She breast-fed her baby for two days before the virus attacked her brain and her heart. They talked about possible blood transfusions or hysterectomy. We had no say-so. Only her husband had say-so. He wouldn't permit surgery or transfusions because they were Jehovah's Witnesses. We really don't know if it would have helped or not. There was a 30 percent chance that she would have survived. She died three days after having her baby.

Not long after my brother and sister died, my grandmother died. That really broke my mom up. My uncle started her on heroin to help her cope with all the loss. She didn't know what she was doing. I was upset with her about it because I thought my mom was going to be the one who made cookies for everyone. She had always been my best friend, but now everything changed.

I was angry at God for a long time after my sister died. I was on a downward spiral, stealing cars, getting high, just doing whatever to ease the pain. After three weeks, I had to turn myself in. It was a way for me to clean up. I was 18 so they offered me the choice of going to the Youth Authority. I told the judge I didn't want to go there because I'd be dealing with a bunch of young knuckleheads. Instead, I went to prison and served 18 months of the two-year sentence.

I learned a lot when I was in prison. When I was growing up, the song of the family was the voices of my siblings getting ready for the day. The song is whatever noises you wake to every morning. This song changes. When I went to jail, it was the sound of the breakfast-cart wheels squeaking as it came down the hall.

The first prison I went to was Chino. Later I was at Soledad and then Tehachapi. That's when jail used to be fun. There was unity among the prisoners from different places. They would back each other up. If there was a child molester out in the yard or somebody was a snitch or a rat, the oldest and wisest would decide the best way to take care of the situation.

Now it's just a manipulation game where the smarter ones manipulate those who are less wise and the strong manipulate the weak. I believe the change came about because of the police on the streets and the guards in the prisons. It was behavior modification. They knew that if we were fighting each other, we wouldn't be fighting them.

I heard of this concept when I got out of prison at age 20 and was visiting my aunt and uncle in Lake Tahoe. I was smoking a joint and my uncle saw me. He said, "So you just got out and you are a *sureño* [southerner] now?"

I said, "That's right. Yup."

He asked, "What are the north and south fighting over?"

"A pair of shoes."

"You guys are stupid!"

We reacted with, "What? What are you talking about?"

"You know that they are in control of you guys. The Hispanic population had control in the prison population, so they cut you in half. The blacks had the Bloods and the Crips, the whites could go anywhere. Now they have the *sureños* and *norteños* fighting each other."

After I got out and finished my three years of parole, my ex moved with me up to Sacramento. I was there several years in the '80s and '90s. During this time, my younger brother died in a car accident. He was only 18. I didn't want to use PCP anymore, so I started doing cocaine and then crack cocaine. That really dragged me to the floor.

I had my first daughter. We had two daughters that were two years apart so they could go to school together. Later, she had an abortion and I fell on my knees, crying, and asking God for forgiveness for that. I thought it was just a procedure, but later thought, "That could have been one of my sons!" I felt it was like sacrificing the baby to the pagan god Moloch.

I opened up a couple chop shops, cutting up cars and selling car parts until I got busted up there about a year later. I got four years for that. I served 34 months.

It was during my time in prison in Sacramento that I got my GED. My mom and dad had also moved to Sacramento. She was working for the state and helped a lot of the family to work for the state. When I got out, I took a few classes at Sac City College and then even I was working for the state.

Before I got out of prison the first time, the jailer told me, "You can never go to college. You can never get a degree." At that time, I believed him. Even though I took a few classes, I was not able to complete a degree.

I was on parole at the same time. One day my cousin stole a shirt. They found out I was on parole and charged me with contributing to the delinquency of a minor and petty theft. So I lost my state job. I had three daughters by that time.

I served four months at Deuel Vocational Institute [closed down now] in Tracy for that. Interestingly, my dad was also serving time in that same prison while I was there. After I got out, I went back to LA. That was in 1995.

I did a lot of drinking and driving. To me it was like a video game. I had lost my brothers and my sister, so I played with death. I figured if it was my turn to go, it was my turn to go.

One day in 1996, I drove straight into a tree at 120 mph off the 10 freeway. The motor ended up just next to me on my left.

They took me to General Hospital. I looked up and saw my grandma and my brother. I looked down and saw myself on the operating table. Then I looked around, and I was on an Indian reservation. I couldn't believe it. I was touching a teepee and smelling smoke. I thought, "This is cool!" At the same time, I felt something bad was trying to get me, but that I was safe on Indian land.

Then I ended up back in my mom and dad's truck. They were arguing and said, "You can't come home, Gilbert."

I thought, "Wait a minute. This can't be happening. My dad is in prison." It kept changing. I went through my childhood and all kinds of stuff.

They say you can't hear things when you are in a coma, but I did hear things, two days before I opened my eyes: "Come on, Gilbert! Come on! Wake up!"

I thought, "Shut up, already!" Eventually, my eyes popped open. I could not talk because I had a hole in my neck. I was about 110 pounds.

They said, "You might not walk again." I wondered if I would ever recover.

Well, I did recover, and I did walk again. I had faith and hope from the spiritual vision I experienced.

Even so, I was still involved in drugs and crime. In 1997, I was stabbed. The next year, I was shot. Each time, I prayed to Jesus for my recovery.

My mom broke her knee and wrist in 2000. She got staph in the hospital and died. That was when I was 33. Even though my dad would beat her, they had stayed together and worked it out.

It wasn't until 2015 that I hit bottom. It was my 48th birthday and I was spending it in jail. I was really down because my wife left me, and my life was such a mess. Every time I argued with her, I would go out and get high.

In jail, I decided to go to church. I figured, "If a guy was coming into the jail to preach to us, he must have something to say." He did. I made a sober and conscious decision to be done with the cycle of drugs and prison. I kept going to church while I was in jail. There was a reason why—it helped me to change my life.

My dad was still smoking crack. Right after I got out of jail for the last time, he died alone in his room. There are things that happen that can make a family stronger.

As Dr. Phil says, "You can't change what you don't acknowledge." After I got out, I knew I had to change. I went back to my wife, mainly to be with the kids and family. I didn't go through any twelve-step program. It was a combination of my experiences in church and what I learned in jail that helped me turn around. The things of the flesh will take you by force, but the Holy Spirit will take you by invitation. You've got to surrender.

In addition to quitting drugs, I wanted to go to college. I would go to the campus to sign up, but then chicken out in the parking lot. The fourth time I tried, I finally got the courage to go in and do it.

I have been a student at East LA College since 2018, taking courses to be a drug counselor. Because of my schooling, I was able to get a job at a rehab home as a counselor.

My kids ask me, "Dad, why did you choose drugs over us?"

I ask them to imagine that your life is going well, and your sister passes away. You pick out her clothes for the casket and go to the funeral. Everyone is there. Then your life starts getting better and two years down the line, your other sister passes.

"Dad, I don't want to think like that!"

"Yeah, well that's my life: death after death after death. It's like a roller coaster and you want to get off!" I wish I had had some grief counseling back then, but I didn't. I turned to drugs to numb myself out.

I started with PCP, then cocaine. I didn't use heroin until I was 28. That was while I was in the county jail. Thankfully, I'm through with drugs and living a better life.

Now I have seven daughters and my youngest just started at UCLA with a GPA of 4.12 from Montebello High School. She got accepted to four colleges and UCLA was her best bet. Everyone was crying, but it was a good cry. Usually, when someone left the house in my family, it was because they went to jail or the morgue.

Growing up, my mom was Catholic and took us to church at Easter and Christmas. She taught us to make the sign of the cross whenever we passed a Catholic church. But now I realize that it's not what religion you are that matters. It's your relationship with God that counts. Here's where I disagree with the twelve-step program where they say, "Your higher power." That leaves room for a highest power and for you to make your own golden calf in your head. You need to "get all the Egypt out of you" and build your relationship with God.

My family up in Paso Robles went through a period of drugs, gangs, and jail. Later, we all cleaned up and are doing well now. Just because your life starts out bad, doesn't mean it has to end up bad. Thanks to Jesus for giving us the keys to the Kingdom. There are blessings for obedience and curses for disobedience. Everything has a lesson if you pay attention.

My goal right now is to work with the youth. They look at going to the Youth Authority as a badge of honor. I want to help them avoid that. These guys in juvenile hall have no guidance or mentors. If they go to prison as young adults with their moms still taking care of them, the older ones will tell them, "You gotta kick in! You gotta start paying money!"

They would ask, "What are you talking about? I came to jail to relax!" They have no clue! They need to see where their lives are going and where they will end up.

I want to be there to help. Like author Jon Acuff said, "Sometimes God redeems your story by surrounding you with people who need to hear your past, so it doesn't become their future."

The Hero in Me

by Gilbert Godinez

You were.
You were my love;
You were my life.
I treated you better than my wife.
I valued you more than my life.
I gave you my time.
I loved you wholeheartedly; we were inseparable.
We slept together; I couldn't wake without you.
You knew me well.
We grew together.
You comforted me through my worst tragedies.
You truly understood the
"Hero in me."
We got along so well.
You were my best friend, my pal.
We laughed. We cried.
You held me tight and told me,
"I'll make everything alright!"
You were true to your word,
Like when you said,
"I'll always be there for you,"
That you knew what I was going through.
It never crossed my mind, there would be a price.
You treated me like a king, when life
Gave me its scorpion sting.
You were my strength when I was weak.
You gave me courage when I lacked confidence.
I never realized you were
Adding up a bill that would cost me
God's greatest gift, my free will.

When I couldn't afford the lifestyle, we adored,
You were eagerly waiting to show me your double-edged
sword.
All in all, after realizing, living, experiencing, and
seeing your true colors,
I still spent many years and countless tears
Trying to capture the closeness we once shared.
After all this, you still had me believing that the
"Hero in me"
Would succeed!
After giving my best and almost selling my soul,
doing everything I detest,
I still couldn't blame you.
After all, it wasn't you who put those bullets in my
gun.
As I raised it to my head,
you really had me believing I was better off dead.
It really seemed the more I cried, the more you lied!
You dragged me through the dirt, just to see me hurt.
It seemed to bring you joy to watch me bounce
around
Like a child's toy.
After grieving and believing the life I was living was
truly my hand of fate
Only to learn that you are nothing but my hurt,
evolved into hate.
After giving you 30 years of my life, it was only by
God's good grace
That I was enlightened with your true name:
"Heroin Me."

Gilbert Godinez

12. Gilbert in 2021

9 ERIC PRITCHARD

I never understood the true meaning of the word freedom, yet I fought for years to achieve it.

My journey in life started with constant abuse, torment, and poverty for me and my two brothers. Those stressed me out and caused me to hate injustice— at least ones done to me. I never reached out to anyone in authority because I had been taught that you don't talk to those people. When nothing was done about the abuse I experienced, I realized that no one was going to protect me. I began to get into fights in school.

I grew up in a household where drug use was normal. My time with cigarettes and coffee was so short that I scarcely remember it. I must've moved to marijuana and beer by about age 10. For me, drugs became an escape from perpetual loneliness and the abusive life I was in.

When caught by my parents, I was initially punished. Eventually my mother gave me permission to smoke and drink within the household because she wanted me to be safe and not be out in the streets.

Plagued by apprehension and a constant fear of what might happen to me next, I was a scared little boy. I didn't have enough energy or ability to concentrate.

In the early 2000s, meth hit my neighborhood like a bomb. A friend introduced me to it when I was just 12 years old.

Methamphetamine changed everything. It allowed me a moment of freedom from the stress. I felt like I had all the energy in the world. It helped me stay awake for days.

Unfortunately, it also led to my craving it more and contributed to my criminality and frequent incarceration. I, like most of my neighboring teenagers, dove deep into meth. Before we knew it, we were all joining gangs and committing crimes.

By 14, my friends and I were having our reunions in detention camps and juvenile hall run by the California Department of Corrections.

Meth led to acid, but meth was the only drug that increased my energy and alleviated the emotional pain that overwhelmed me daily.

The truth is that meth only masked my problems. I quickly found I could not function without it. Though meth temporarily alleviated my emotional distress, it also increased the hopelessness I felt. Thus, it created a cycle of abusive thoughts and led to further reliance on the drug.

This way of living got me a life sentence in the California State Prison system at the age of 14. For the next 21 years, I struggled with the very idea of freedom—this elusive condition which I had let slip away at such a young age. Now it seemed to have a completely negative hold on my life.

Thankfully, the people of California, through their legislative representatives, had the compassion and wisdom to provide personal assistance for prisoners. Nine years of recovery education with programs like AA, NA, and substance abuse treatments helped me to understand my potential for real change.

Though these are all commonly known as self-help programs, I prefer to call them "self-abuse treatments." As the saying goes, if drugs were the problem, then we could just lock up the drugs and we wouldn't have any problems. Unfortunately, we human beings are flawed from within.

It took 15 years for me to finally wake up and see that I was the one keeping myself in chains. It was this realization that caused me to develop skills which would change my life forever.

Of course, my only true path to freedom was hard work and dedication to my own recovery. It took changing myself completely to see that freedom was indeed real and obtainable. Changing my own perspective was what gave true freedom.

In prison, I also had cognitive behavioral therapy (CBT). That gave me the ability to direct my life in an orderly manner. Freedom without self-restraint is chaos. In the past, I typically only knew of two emotions: happiness and anger. CBT taught me how to identify the other emotions and how to deal with them. When I developed a better recognition of these emotions and the situations that evoked them, I was able to understand my role in choosing drugs and a self-abusive lifestyle. I applied these concepts to my religious journey as well. I found clarity and am no longer using any type of drug.

Through years of serving my fellow inmates as a group facilitator and co-facilitator of a substance abuse program, I learned that freedom comes from the values we attach to things in our lives. That knowledge prompted me to encourage my groups with the old saying, "How do you eat an elephant? One bite at a time."

There were two other things that sped my release. In 2013, CA State Senate Bill 260, Chapter 312 allowed parole, under numerous conditions, for offenders who committed crimes prior to age 18. Then in 2016, SB 261's Fact Sheet provided parole hearings for certain offenders whose attitudes have matured and whose crime was committed under age 26.

Finally, after serving 21 years on a six-years-to-life sentence, I was given a date to be released: September 29, 2016.

The days leading up to my release were nerve-racking. Everyone, many of whom were more excited than I was, asked how much time I had left, what I was going to do, and what my first meal would be. It all began to be a bother. For a small moment, I revisited those months of self-doubt.

I instantly remembered the bits-at-a-time metaphor and I calmed down. Getting out was the first problem. I could do nothing from prison, so why stress? "Wait until I'm out."

On September 28th, I was filled with anxiety and fear. I tried to excuse it as nerves, but it was fear. I had fallen once before in this world. I couldn't allow myself to do it again.

September 29th finally came, and the day started off badly. I didn't receive a parole ducat from the assignment office. [Note: A ducat is an appointment slip and movement authorization allowing a prisoner to move around the prison without escort.] I thought to myself, "What's wrong now?"

At 10 a.m., my cell door finally opened. The officer called my name.

"I got bad news for you," he said.

"Yeah, what's up?" I asked.

"You're going home," he said, "and that's bad news for us because we're losing one of our best programmers."

I jumped off my bed, prayed with my roommates, and smiled the whole way to the R&R room where for the first time in 21 years, I put on real clothes, my own clothes. I sat there and smiled—numb from the inside out, telling myself no matter what, I will make it and stay determined.

As I walked closer and closer to the electrified fences, my heart beat against my chest and I felt like I wanted to cry and laugh at the same time. It was amazing when I reached the final step out of prison. "Last pat down," the officer at the gate said.

The first steps into freedom did not take long. A van was waiting just inches away. I got in and did not look back.

My mother once told me, "If you never want to see the places you've been, then don't ever look back when you leave." So I faced forward with my cheesy smile and new clothes.

I rode from that van to another that took me to a residential, substance-abuse program in San Jose, California. The ride was awful because I got motion sickness; I hadn't ridden in a car in 21 years. It wasn't long before my head was spinning. Four to five stops later, we finally pulled into the driveway of my new living arrangement.

I know I left out what the world looked like to me, because, honestly, for most of the ride, my head was down with my eyes covered. I didn't really get a good look. It was just a couple of green trees and new cars— and my stupid smile.

When I finally got out of the van, it took about 10 minutes for my head to stop spinning. But when it did— wow, what a beautiful sight. I stood still for a moment, looked all around, then walked up to the nearest tree. I ran my hand over the bark. The feeling was amazing and empowering as it touched the tips of my fingers. It felt…well, …barky. It was rough against my fingers. I thanked God for the pleasure. I picked up a leaf and crumbled it in my hand. I had thought of these simple sensations for years. Now it was finally happening.

In the background, I could hear the intake staff gathering all my information for placement. I cursed the idea of that never-forgiving, never-forgetting part of my life. But without any hesitation, I walked up to the program staff and confidently introduced myself. I felt no insecurity. I knew who I was now and that I would never allow myself to be subject to another man again.

As I experienced their orientation process, I laughed to myself, but only because I had done this very process with hundreds of clients while working as an orientation clerk in prison. I filled out my papers, feeling like the pro I am. How wonderful it was to hear that I would be able to call home. Countless members of my family and friends had already contacted them, inquiring about my stay at the half-way house.

The first person I called was my mother. The pure joy in her voice almost brought the professional staff and me to tears. My greatest fear while in prison was that I'd still be there when my mother passed away—before she could see the new me. During those hardest days in prison, when my old thinking and nature would rear its head, I would think of my mother to regain strength.

I will be honest. The process for gaining my freedom was not easy for me. Many of the people supervising me had never dealt with an ex-lifer before and were not fully prepared for the things I needed. Most of the people in the program were never in prison, especially from such a young age as I had been. They already had an ID, Social Security number, and a myriad of other life experiences like getting a job or even just ordering food for themselves at a fast-food restaurant. I needed someone to help me with all of these.

Nevertheless, the personal, moral values and ethics that I gained while in prison allowed me to excel at everything. I quickly got my California ID, a job, and a bank account—all things I had never had before.

One of the most touching moments of my new freedom came in relation to my touching of that tree bark on my first day of physical freedom. A friend and I were talking, and she was sharing how unhappy she was with her life. I stopped her as I saw that she was reaching a level that was going to become hurtful to her.

"Stop," I said, "Come with me."

"Where we going?" she asked.

"Just come," I responded.

She came with quiet anticipation. I led her to one of the trees in the surrounding parking lot.

"Touch the tree," I said.

"Why?" she asked.

"Just touch the tree," I said, "and I will tell you." She touched the tree.

"OK," she asked, "Now what?"

"What did you feel?" I asked.

"A tree," she said.

"No, I mean what did it feel like?" I questioned.

"Bark," she said.

"And what does bark feel like?" I asked.

"I don't know," she said.

"Don't you get it?" I asked, "This tree has substance. It is alive and has texture to it."

"OK. So, what's the point?" she asked.

"The point is," I said, "this tree is something that helps us every day, yet no one ever notices this tree—unless one day it becomes rare. No one ever touches the tree and... appreciates it. We are like trees. We go through our lives and, for a lot of us, no one ever notices us. We may be alone, though we are completely surrounded. But then, one day, someone comes along and touches us. Then everything is different."

"This," I said, "is the opportunity we are given every day—to touch someone's life in a way that will allow them to feel alive."

It has been a few years now since I walked out of prison. I can say with well-grounded conviction that the world is a beautiful place and that grateful freedom is the best way to experience it.

Like most people, I have had to work very hard with little help, but it has only proven to me that I have the capabilities to survive in the same world I left. It's the same world, but I meet it with a completely changed mindset. Today, I have a car that I paid for myself, a job that will become a career for me, and even bigger dreams—the sort which I have not had in a long time.

I share my story to allow others to see that they are not alone and that they can find help if they want it.

As a person with a meth addiction, I now choose to rely on treatment rather than any substance to alleviate any problems that might arise in my life. I suggest that others do the same, because methamphetamine is a powerful drug and the damage it causes is too great. Put simply: "Don't meth around with that stuff."

I encourage everyone to realize that we are all capable of greatness, but too often fear intervenes. Do not fear to seek help. We are all waiting for someone to say, "Hello." Sometimes we must say it first, as a first step to freedom.

All we need to do is step outside of the norm and touch a tree or *become* a tree in order to help someone else reach freedom. The first prison I was ever in was the one inside my own head.

13. Eric in School Band and in 2021 with Hilary

10 GARY GARZA

I don't know for sure—can I even trust the people who were there? They say that I was born September 7th, 1964, in White Memorial Hospital, East Los Angeles. Though I was born in East LA, by the time I started school, we were living in neighboring Pico Rivera.

In the communities and neighborhoods where I've lived in East Los Angeles and Pico Rivera, discrimination by the Los Angeles County Sheriff's department was running rampant. When I was very young in the late '60s and early '70s, essentially everyone in these communities was affected by the presumption that all young Hispanic men were gang members. The police looked at all of us as bad people.

It sounds funny to say so today, but the people were more afraid of the police than the gangs on their block. As a young boy, I learned really quickly that the police were not our friends.

One day I was riding my bike up the street from my house to what we called the dairy to get some bathroom tissue. As I was riding, I was cut off by a police car. When they stopped me, the two big white policemen got out of their car, threw my bike to the ground, picked me up, shoved me onto the police car, put their hands onto my private parts, and pulled my pockets inside-out while rubbing their hands up and down the backs of my legs. Then they pushed my face into the hood of the police car and asked me what I was doing and where I was going so fast on my bike.

As my face was smashed onto the hood of the car, I could not see straight and could barely speak. I answered them in a squeaky voice, "I am going to the dairy for my mother, for toilet paper, sir. She needs it right now!"

The police officer said, "Sure you are. You're running drugs aren't you?"

I said, "No sir, I'm just going for toilet paper."

Then they put their handcuffs on me and rammed me into their car, saying, "Where d'ja steal the bike?" I was scared; I started to cry, but they didn't care. I sat in the car for ten minutes. Finally, they took me out of the car and let me go on my way. All in one moment this had changed my life forever.

Until then, I always valued the law, but law enforcement needs to be reviewed and changed for the betterment of the people's rights. We are people of love and compassion who love our family and friends.

Of course, I must admit that I was no angel. At age 10, I obtained a small amount of cocaine from someone in the neighborhood. I soon had plenty of access and was making friends by passing the stuff around. By the time I was in high school, things had really gotten out of hand.

A year or so into my high school, about age 15, my father started a truck unloading service. He gathered independent workers from the streets and offered them a job to work for $300 a week. The competition paid only $100 a week. So instead of fighting him, they worked for him.

He did so well that he converted into a trucking business. He didn't know anything about trucking, but he didn't care. He got a deal and bought three bobtail trucks. He started a little transportation company. He later bought more trucks and did pretty well.

He eventually got into the wine distribution business across Southern California. My dad and my brother are the ones who did the work. By then, I was too messed up with cocaine to work for them. The times they gave me a chance, they had to fire me. But it's amazing how much a kid can learn about the business world with the piecemeal exposure I had.

At 15, I was totally committed to drugs and crime. None of my high school teachers cared enough to speak to me, much less intervene. I walked out of high school with no diploma and into the arms of an unobservant world. The only time the world lifted its head was to catch me doing something it had banned.

The attention I got was a series of legal detentions.

As I grew older, I got into other kinds of drugs, like LSD. I first tried heroin in my 30s. I was doing speedballs—cocaine and heroin at the same time. I didn't like the high of the heroin by itself. It would make me throw up and I didn't like lying on the floor, high and sick, a condition which I call "all f'ed up." It was better combined with cocaine.

Later, I started smoking cocaine. That was really bad. I would do a little bit here and there. This made the truckers limit me from moving up in my own dad's company. Though they fired me again and again, I became more and more business savvy.

Then I would go back to my street homies and hang out. Most of them were gang members, but I was never in a gang myself.

I was doing one crime after another and running up a long rap sheet. The earliest crime I can recall was when I was 12. I was into shoplifting, so I went to Woolworth's and stole sunglasses—25 pairs.

I kept using cocaine, crack, and heroin and doing all sorts of crimes. Guns were always at my side. I found myself in city and county jails—maybe 13 times.

My older brother lucked out; he met a girl whom he loved. When he made her pregnant, she wanted the baby. He had the good sense to listen to her advice. He ignored the lure of drugs, shouldered his responsibilities, and has been a good citizen to the present day.

In December 1991 at age 27, I ended my career with crack cocaine. In January 1992, I went into rehab for one year at the Salvation Army in Pasadena. Once I got out, I was sober for a few years. I started work at Albertsons and worked my way up to supervisor. That lasted for eight years.

I did so well at Albertsons that they made me a foreman. That might sound good, but by then I was starting on meth. My boss liked that I was able to work really fast and efficiently. Part of my job was to get the whole workforce to work equally fast by all taking meth.

At least I was functional. In the midst of all that, when I was 30 in '94, I met and married a delightful and beautiful girl named Yolanda from Guadalajara. My family all chipped in to help us buy a house. My dad put in 10K so that I was able to buy a home in Ontario, CA in '95. We sold that in 2000 and used the money to buy a condo in the city of Commerce.

Things seemed good until my wife divorced me in 2001. She had gotten what she wanted: her citizenship, a lot of money, and her master's degree.

I fell apart. I started heavily into meth and became suicidal.

As my addiction to meth got worse, I was talking to trees and shooting at poles. I even tried to shoot myself—a glancing shot to my head. I landed in Long Beach State Hospital on a 5150 designation: "a danger to myself and others."

After I was released, I got involved with gangs with whom I was committing various types of fraud. We had quite an operation going, making fake birth certificates, IDs, and counterfeit money for about five years.

That's where my experience working for my dad came in handy. I had learned how to use the internet and how to do banking transactions.

The internet was not well known in the early 2000s. Nor did it have the safeguards it now has. It was easy for us to go online and buy computers and cell phones using peoples' stolen ID information. For example, we could buy six cell phones at a time. Then we would wait for

USPS to bring the stuff to the peoples' homes. It would be left at the doorstep, and we would do whatever it took to get it. Then we could use the phones or sell them for cash. That's how we got money to get high.

I personally did not like to steal from people who were struggling and trying to get ahead. I preferred to steal from big companies that had a lot of money and had insurance. We would get peoples' checking account information and have checks printed with their account numbers.

I won't mention the sneaky ways we did that and how we wrote and cashed checks. But by the time the companies got on the ball, we would have spent the money already. The companies didn't know who we were, only that they got hit. We would survive on the money, paying our bills, buying food, and buying dope with whatever was left.

At the end of 2007, the FBI arrested me for counterfeiting and for selling the stolen phones that we used for our work. I was put on probation for three years. They told me that if I did the three years, they would drop the charges. I lasted three months. I got high, went to an auto parts store, and fixed a car for a guy there in the parking lot. He wanted to give me a ride home, but it was a small 2-door car, and I was so big and heavy that I would not be able to jump out if needed. So, I refused the ride.

He insisted that I would be insulting him. Reluctantly, I got into the back seat since he had someone else in the front. Sure enough, we got stopped by the cops who found marijuana, cocaine, meth, counterfeit money, a gun, and bullets in the car. I got five felonies right there.

Because I was just in the car and had only helped those guys out by fixing the car, I got probation. However, the dealer signed an affidavit saying the drugs were mine. That meant I got the lump of the charges and the dealer got away with no charges.

During my probation, a friend came over and I got in the car with him to go to Frys. I didn't know it, but the guy I came with was stealing things. As we walked out of the store, he started ripping open packages and stuffing things into his shirt. We got jumped by security.

I was bigger and stronger than the security men, so I fought back and beat them up. Eventually, enough of them subdued me. I insisted that I had paid for my things. The cameras confirmed that, but since I was with the thief, they blamed me too. It turned out to be a parole violation because I was with someone during a crime.

Starting on December 25, 2008, because of my long criminal history and many stints in city and county jails, I finally made it to the big time. My prize was a three-year, free tour of the State of California—on my way to three of the state's 34 prisons. My first year was in the LA County Jail (LACJ)—just a warmup.

Then I was transferred to the California Institution for Men (a.k.a., Chino State Prison) about 20 miles northeast of Disneyland. I could really feel the closeness—and similarities.

Entering the prison system requires processing and evaluation which typically takes several months. They say to expect four months. Whatever it was, I felt I became well-acquainted with Chino.

They evaluated me as having congestive heart failure. That had developed by age 44 due to my lifestyle and lifelong obesity on top of the drugs I'd done and liquor I'd consumed. They put me into Wasco State Prison for a year. Wasco is about 20 miles north of Bakersfield. It had a medical unit which I needed.

At that time, the water system there was so poor that it was running dirt-colored water three or four days a week. It happened that part of my background included having a certificate in water treatment. Thus, I knew how to rig a filtering system which the men loved. Of course, it required me to rip up lots of our $10 sheets to keep making the crucial filters. Then I would sell the clean water to the guys for candy, cigarettes, and the money which some received in their monthly care packages.

Over the course of a year, we used a lot of sheets. It was easier to rip up more sheets than to wash the filters. After all, we might be in prison, but we don't do laundry.

For the sheets I received a considerable bill. What do you think I did with that?

Fellow Wasco alumni have made Internet comments. One said, "Great place to get in touch with your inner self. Join one of the many social clubs. Lots of activities and helpful staff."

Another reminisced, "Good view. The food wasn't bad, but I did find a shank in it one time and nearly choked. The inmates were a pretty cool group though. They only tried to stab me three times during my stay. Overall—a 5-star experience."

My last assignment was to Norco for another year. It too was chosen with an eye to my medical needs. Though Norco was back near Chino, to get there, I took a different route. I got a totally new view of the California desert. I settled within a mile of the concrete-encased Santa Ana River. I've never been able to see if it has any trout.

While I was in LACJ, my mom got Alzheimer's and was staying with my sister Kathy in Montebello. My father, who was remarried, was still living in our long-time family home in Pico Rivera.

In spite of my sheet larceny, I was so well-behaved that they paroled me in January 2011. I was paroled to my dad's Pico Rivera home and started working as a driver for his business. Soon I was driving him around because his diabetes made him almost blind. Getting more responsibilities in the business, I was dealing with customers and doing really well.

It was not long before dad got very sick and had to move in with Kathy in Montebello. He also wanted me to be with him. That left the Pico Rivera home vacant.

We rented it out to some family members. They threw out all my things. Then they left without paying rent. That was tough.

I got my parole moved to Montebello where my sister kept an eye on me. Because of all the help my sister gave me, the parole officer said, "As long as you are with your sister, I know you are doing well. The day you are no longer with your sister, we will throw you back in prison." Because of her, I was released from parole after only two years.

Kathy's husband, my brother-in-law, took over the trucking business after my dad retired. I stayed to work with him. We did well for three years, until my health started failing. When my dad died and the market was bad, we could no longer afford to maintain the company. We lost it to our creditors.

By 2017, I was 420 pounds, 53 years old, and finally had to retire.

I've known Gilbert Vasquez most of my life. He's co-founder of the East Los Angeles College (ELAC) Homeboy Scholars club with Adrian Caceres. We did high school together in the early '80s. He was selling weed while I was the cocaine kid. I lost track of him for a while after he was caught selling to an undercover officer.

A couple of decades later, Gilbert encouraged me to not just sit and do nothing, but to go to school and get a degree. Degrees are like steppingstones in the adult world—like a high school diploma or a GED certificate is the last big step out of childhood when we are about 18 years old.

I didn't want to go back to drugs, so I went to college. I started at ELAC in 2017. At first, I took every athletic course they had: swimming, running, weightlifting, etc. I lost 100 pounds during five semesters. Then I started taking book courses and decided to major in psychology. I would take two hard classes and one easy athletic class. This gave me the boost I needed to get back into being a student.

By the time I started at ELAC, I had many skills from my diverse life experiences, but I never anticipated where they would lead me in an academic institution. I've traded one form of institutionalization for another.

A funny thing happened when I first arrived at ELAC. I joined the Associated Student Union and soon was made a senator. I then received the opportunity to be on the board.

As a board member, I learned that ELAC is just one of the nine large campuses of the Los Angeles Community College District. I didn't realize that ELAC, with an enrollment of 35,000 students, is the largest college in the whole district.

In that position, I was put in charge of the South Gate Campus to help students get involved in college and enjoy campus life. I have talked before thousands of students. I tell them how to express the leader they all have inside themselves. They have been running with it. We've started three clubs: the Omni Club, Child Development Club, and Psychology Club South.

I also got into the Male Leadership Academy (MLA) at ELAC. They showed me that we men of color are powerful people in our leadership capabilities. After one year I was made President of the club. Soon the Academy was closing due to no funding. We kept the club going anyway.

Noticing that being a leader wasn't limited to just men, I started talking to women's groups. I talked to the MLA board and changed the name of our club. We are now called the Alumni Leadership Club (ALC) to include women. We've helped many students to sharpen their skills; they have become positive and confident leaders. Many have graduated to attend several different universities.

Today I'm still helping many students with their life problems. I do this by the example of my life. My goal is to help as many students as possible to find their confidence and be the best they can possibly be.

Since my mental health is good, I only had to go into the mental ward once in my decades of incarceration. The doctors have said I am OK, though I have had a lot of trauma in my life. They said I should just try to relax and not let things get to me.

At ELAC I have been an A student for three years and will soon have four Associate of Arts (AA) degrees. They are in the fields of psychology, general education, administration of justice, and sports management.

I am also working as a counselor to help the same population from which I came. I will go to a university to get both a Bachelor of Arts (BA) and a Master of Arts (MA) degree in psychology and counseling.

I got away with a lot in my past and now I'm paying the penance. I have changed my life and don't want to hurt anyone anymore. I decided to be a college student and am really close to heading for my bachelor's at USC or UCLA, whichever one takes me.

Pray for me that I may be worthy of my new chances. I have been given the opportunity to revise my life and encourage others to change theirs.

14. Gilbert Vasquez, Gary, Phyllis, Ricardo, and Hilary, 2019

ACKNOWLEDGEMENTS

There are many who have contributed in one way or another to the making of this book. What I must say first of all is that I am deeply grateful for the privilege of being asked and being allowed to help give it birth. The men in this book all have such busy lives with work, school, and family obligations. I appreciate their taking the time and making the efforts to share their stories.

Thanks especially to Adrian Caceres and Gilbert Vasquez for their work with the Homeboy Scholars club at East LA College (ELAC). They have been closest to our contributors to encourage the homies to get started in college and to persist therein. They were first in encouraging me to edit and assemble these stories into book form. They connected me with many of the club members.

We all thank Dr. Lisa Vartanian and Dr. Lou Hughes who wrote a grant which continues to fund the Addiction Studies Program at ELAC. The program has 260 students in 2021 and a set of wrap-around and case management services for Former or Currently Incarcerated Students, hence the acronym FOCIS.

I am grateful to Chaplain Russell Martin who connected me with Steven Gonzales and acted as a liaison for communication and transferring documents to and from Steven who is an inmate in the Richard J. Donovan Correctional Facility. Thanks also go to Rebecca Kroll who took over as liaison after Russell was transferred to another facility.

My wife and I are thankful to Jesus "Chucho" Ruiz of *Chicanos por la Causa* in Tucson for putting us in touch with Roberto Rodriguez, PhD. We are thankful to Dr. Rodriguez, of the University of Arizona in Tucson for putting us in touch with Jose Cortez of Phoenix, whose story we are happy to include in this anthology.

It is an honor to have Fr. Greg Boyle, the founder of Homeboy Industries, write the foreword for this book. His organization has been an amazing support to countless homies. Many, including myself, owe him a debt of gratitude. His latest (2021) book is *The Whole Language: The Power of Extravagant Tenderness*.

Thanks also to all the others at Homeboy Industries who support the homeboys directly and who have encouraged my wife and me:

> Todd Carter greeted us when we arrived. He was eager to help us find the people we came to see.

> Lio Camarillo was the capable Navigator who assisted us in lining up meetings.

> Hector Verdugo, Fr. Greg's right-hand man and Associate Executive Director, was kind enough to meet with us and encouraged our efforts.

Brittany Morton greases all the parts of the very-professionally-run organization. She heads the Pathways to College program (see Arthur Nides' story).

Laura Hayes helps the homies at the high school level as the Academic Program Coordinator.

Fr. Mark Torres has been encouraging to me and said, "I continue to pray that your project is fruitful."

Of course, this book would not have been possible without Phyllis, my amazing wife who used her computer skills to keep track of the status of each story through every step of the process. She put all the stories into a formatted file for publication. She was my editorial assistant and moral support.

Thank you to all our wonderful proof readers who took their time in the busy Christmas season to go through proof copies and helped us make the final version the best possible: Jose Cortez (whose story also appears), Ron DeBlanc, Ana Lopez, and Brandon Cortez.

ABOUT THE AUTHOR

Paul McGuire had a classical education taught by Benedictine monks at St. Gregory's High School and College in Oklahoma. He joined the faculty as Brother Hilary, named after the famed Bishop Hilary of Poitiers, France.

Brother Hilary was always looking for ways to broaden the lives of his students. In 1970, he was moved by a production in Texas to create his own theatrical version of the rock opera *Tommy* by permission of The Who. It was like the music videos of today with the actors adding dance and drama to the music. *Tommy* was first professionally produced by the Seattle Opera in 1971.

After ten years teaching math and tennis in Oklahoma, Hilary was sent to teach math and literature in East LA. He started a National Junior Tennis League team in his spare time. Local Chicano gang members joined his private school students and learned discipline the fun way. At the same time, he founded the tennis team at Cantwell High School in nearby Montebello.

Two years later, Hilary was reassigned to OK. There he developed a line of unique and philosophical sculptures, employing the medium of antique iron from Oklahoma farm equipment and railroad steel. These are reflective of his philosophy background and the approach he uses in teaching math. His most notable piece *Justice?* appeared in a full-page photo with the artist in *Southwest Art* magazine, March 1977.

Inspired by his work with the gangs in East LA, this sculpture represents the alternatives of justice as a trap, chains, or a hook. Then if one gets out of those, the blacksmith tongs await below. "Many homies," Hilary says, "feel that they have only such negative alternatives in their lives."

In recent years, Hilary has shown *Justice?* along with many others in two San Diego exhibits and has been approached for an exhibit of ten sculptures at the Oklahoma Hall of Fame. You can see them on his website by entering the shortcut **bit.ly/hpmcguire** in any browser.

After leaving the monastic life, Hilary Paul McGuire taught math 37 years for the San Diego Community College District. Since retiring, he has been tutoring math and teaching tennis to local youth. He met his wife of 39 years on a tennis court in San Diego. They have three grown children and still enjoy playing tennis together. Their motto is, "There's not much we can do for the world, but what we can, we do."

15. Adrian Caceres with Hilary in LA, 2021

16. Brother Hilary with *Justice?* in 1976 at St. Gregory's College

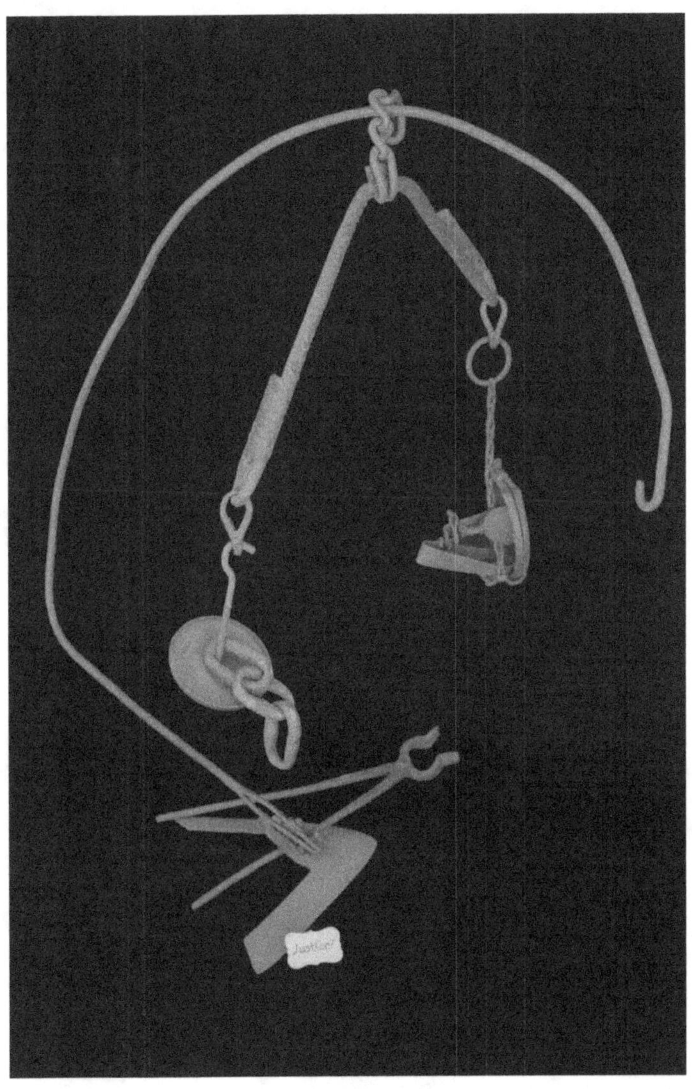

17. *Justice?* in 2018